SURVEYS FOR TOWN AND COUNTRY PLANNING

John N. Jackson

Director, Institute of Land Use,
Brock University, St Catharines, Ontario

formerly Lecturer in Town and
Country Planning, University of Manchester

GREENWOOD PRESS, PUBLISHERS
WESTPORT, CONNECTICUT

Library of Congress Cataloging in Publication Data

Jackson, John N
   Surveys for town and country planning.

   Reprint of the ed. published by Hutchinson University
Library, London, in series: Hutchinson University
library: geography.
   Includes bibliographies and index.
   1. Cities and towns--Planning--1945-   2. Land.
3. Surveying. I. Title.
[HT166.J26 1976]   309.2'62   76-7580
ISBN 0-8371-8866-0

Originally published in 1963 by Hutchinson University
Library, London

Reprinted with the permission of Hutchinson Publishing
Group, Ltd.

Reprinted in 1976 by Greenwood Press,
a division of Williamhouse-Regency Inc.

Library of Congress Catalog Card Number 76-7580

ISBN 0-8371-8866-0

Printed in the United States of America

HC 11-15

To
Kathleen, Andrew,
Susan and Paul

CONTENTS

PREFACE

Town and country planning is concerned with the use and development of land. This book examines the range of information which is required as a basis for policy decisions, and suggests various methods by which this might be collected. No attempt is made either to analyse the facts concerned with a particular aspect of land use or to suggest solutions to current planning issues.

My first debt of gratitude is to the many authorities referred to in the text, and to the ideas from other sources which have doubtless been incorporated unwittingly. I am indebted to Professor R. H. Kinvig and the staff in the Department of Geography, University of Birmingham, for their systematic training in method; to Mr A. R. Duncan, County Planning Officer of Herefordshire, and Mr H. F. Alston, Town Planning Officer of Hull, for the stimulus of applied research into current problems of land use; to the staff and students of the Department of Town and Country Planning, University of Manchester, for the discussion of ideas and their application in field-work, theses and design projects.

Colleagues in the University and in local or national government have commented on the manuscript. Some prefer anonymity because of their official positions. I am glad to thank Mr T. W. Freeman and Professor W. G. East for their initial encouragement and subsequent advice, and Messrs G. F. Chadwick, J. B. Cullingworth, F. Fishwick, F. J. McCulloch, D. F. Medhurst, I. Melville, W. M. Ogden, D. G. Robinson, W. Taylor and R. Turner for their criticisms. My typist, Mrs V. C. Stirling, deserves a special word of thanks. The merits of the book owe much to these people for their respective contributions; its deficiencies remain my own.

Manchester, December 1961   J. N. J.

COPY OF ADVERTISEMENT FOR POST OF
PLANNING ASSISTANT
with names and dates changed

CITY AND COUNTY OF HALLAM
TOWN PLANNING DEPARTMENT

Applications are invited from suitably qualified persons for the post of Planning Assistant. The post is in the Research Section of the Department and preference will be given to candidates possessing an Honours Degree in one of the Social Sciences, including Geography, Economics or Sociology, and/or practical research experience with a Local Authority.

The work is varied in content and involves the detailed study of particular land use, social and economic problems within the City under the guidance of a Senior Planning Assistant (Research).

An up-to-date record is maintained of population, employment, unemployment, building, trade and port statistics, and reports are prepared to indicate current trends with recommendations, where appropriate, as to the course of action which these figures indicate.

Investigations of particular problems provide an important aspect of the work. Projects over the past two years have included:

> An appraisal of Journey to Work by place of work and method of travel.
>
> A survey of Central Area Car Parking both by volume and duration.
>
> An assessment of housing demand in relation to the availability of sites.
>
> A study of delays experienced by vehicles and persons at level crossings.
>
> Sundry road traffic surveys.
>
> An investigation into the requirements of industrialists to be disturbed by redevelopment.
>
> A study of family size and structure in relation to house size.
>
> The productivity of gardens, and the utilization of allotments.
>
> School, shop and other requirements in new residential areas.

Application forms may be obtained from the undersigned and should be returned not later than Saturday 14 April 1962.

J. L. Dates, M.T.P.I., A.R.I.C.S., A.M.I.MUN.E.

Town Planning Officer

Guildhall
Hallam
20 March 1962

1
SURVEYS AND THE PLANNING PROCESS

LAND-USE planning is more than a compound of architecture, engineering, public administration and the social sciences. It is a new and emerging discipline with its own scientific and objective approach to its central theme, the use and development of land. 'City planning may be regarded as a means for systematically anticipating and achieving adjustment in the physical environment of a city consistent with social and economic trends and sound principles of civic design: It involves a continuing process of deriving, organizing and presenting a broad and comprehensive programme for urban development and renewal. It is designed to fulfil local objectives of social, economic and physical well-being, considering both immediate needs and those of the foreseeable future. It examines the economic basis for an urban centre existing in the first place; it investigates its cultural, political, economic and physical characteristics both as an independent entity and as a component of a whole cluster of urban centres in a given region; and it attempts to design a physical environment which brings these elements into the soundest and most harmonious plan for the development and renewal of the urban area as a whole. Land-use planning is a part of this larger process of city planning . . . [it] is basically concerned with the location, intensity and amount of land development required for the various space-using functions of city life.'[1]

The aims of planning

British planning, in its present comprehensive form, is a product of the post-war period. A government White Paper in 1944 stated that 'provision for the right use of land, in accordance with a considered policy, is an essential requirement of the government's programme of post-war reconstruction. New houses . . .; the new lay-out of areas devastated by enemy action or blighted by reason of age or bad living conditions; the new schools which will be required . . .; the balanced distribution of industry . . .; the requirements of a healthy and well-balanced agriculture; the preservation of land for national parks and forests, and the assurance to the people of enjoyment of the sea and countryside in times of leisure; a new and safer highway system better adapted to modern industrial and other needs; the proper provision of air-fields—all these *related parts of a single reconstruction programme* involve the use of land, and it is essential that their various claims on land should be so harmonized as to ensure for the people of this country the greatest possible measure of individual well-being and national prosperity, both in this and in succeeding generations. The government desire to make that achievement possible.'[2]

This official list, compiled during the enthusiasm of war, is not exhaustive. The general planning policy in conurbations is to curb their further physical growth by green belts, to disperse population and industry to new and expanded centres, to control the volume of central area employment and to encourage urban renewal of the inner areas. Since many rural planning authorities are concerned with the devitalizing incidence of depopulation, their proposals may include the strengthening of facilities in the market towns, the provision of adequate houses, schools and water-supply schemes for families living in agricultural districts, and the introduction of selected industries into chosen focal situations. The ubiquitous motor vehicle presents a problem of growing importance involving the routing and construction of motorways, the impact of such roads on the intricate pattern of urban and rural land use, the creation of pedestrian shopping precincts, the provision of off the street access for service vehicles, adequate provision for short- and long-term parking and the thoughtful planning of residential neighbourhoods and of industrial estates.

A powerful segment of the planning profession is concerned with the visual impact of development and with the need to accommodate all new buildings and structures harmoniously within the landscape;

aesthetic and amenity considerations, an innate desire to enhance the beauty and architectural appeal of towns and a conscious attempt to improve the quality of man's living environment are here the driving force. The reorganization of land tenure and the unification of ownership to permit large-scale redevelopment, the attainment of a single administration over conurbations and regions to sponsor an integrated approach to common problems, a reforming zeal to abolish slums or an excessive journey to work, the urge to redevelop land under a more desirable or efficient use, the provision of housing at certain standards to all groups of the population or the elimination of enforced overcrowding inspire the contributions of further specialists within the field of planning.[3]

Many forces, vested and sinister interests, desires and habits, expectations and ambitions, exert pressures on the use of land. The cost of land, its means of development and the financial incidence of renewal may raise complex political issues. Compensation and betterment, green belts, attitudes towards industrial location and the subsidies available for town expansion or high-density residential development provide examples of economic, political as well as planning issues. A decision to restrict immigration or to raise the rate of interest on loan charges will affect land use in Birmingham or defer an extension to a school. A variety of social, moral, psychological and visual pressures make topics such as residential densities, layouts and locations difficult to assess on a purely objective basis. The economic climate, including the proportion of the national resources to be devoted to new highways and the availability or otherwise of a grant in aid of development, exerts consequences on local planning decisions and the phasing and quality of local development. The incentive of a chief official or the calibre of a town's planning committee can exert a vital impact on the form of urban development. Many of these elements are imponderables.

Surveys and national planning

Planning is not always the logical and rational process which provides the theme of this book and which its many proponents would like to see. Thus the Barlow, Scott and Uthwatt reports each recognized the national scope of planning, its comprehensive nature and that its problems cannot be solved either separately or locally. Each report contained a recommendation for a central planning authority 'by which the requirements of agriculture, transport, public services and defence, as well as housing, industrial location, town siting and other matters, can be given proper weight and considered as a whole'.[4] The idea was that the Minister of 'National Development', the term used in the Scott report, should have neither executive powers nor himself be head of a department of state concerned with the use and development of land. His responsibilities at Cabinet level would be to formulate comprehensive, consistent and integrated national policies. Development, the making and execution of plans, and the control of land use would be the concern of other government departments, statutory bodies and local government. As it is, many departments of state have duties which bear upon the use and development of land; each requires (or should require) research staff to examine the implications and repercussions of development, to perceive the relationships which exist between different types of development and to weld these factors into an integrated plan.

The planning section of the Ministry of Housing and Local Government has the responsibility for 'securing consistency and continuity in the framing and execution of a national policy for the use and development of land'.[5] Its planning functions have included the provision of technical advice and assistance to local planning authorities, the preparation of a national series of 1: 625,000 planning maps, technical memoranda (unpublished) on survey subjects, publications on the method of planning and the provision of information on topics such as the projection of population or land with mineral reserves to local planning authorities. It is the ministry's responsibility to approve, modify or reject the local development plans, to determine the major local issues for planning permission and to resolve differences between adjacent planning bodies.

Substantial powers for planning the use and development of land have also been vested with other departments of state. The Board of Trade are responsible to Parliament for national control over the location of industry and have powers to give grants for industrial projects in 'development districts', to restrict development in congested conurbations and to encourage industrial proposals in one locality rather than another. The Ministry of Agriculture are concerned with many problems affecting the rural community, including the choice of land for development, the housing of agricultural workers, land tenure, the improvement of farm holdings, the reclamation of waste land, land drainage and the provision of water supplies on farms. The Ministry of Works control and dispose of all Crown Land, including service establishments and the post office, and are the custodians of ancient monuments and historic buildings. The school building programme, and the land requirements for schools and playing fields, are under the aegis of the Ministry of Education. The Ministry of Transport are responsible for the efficiency of the whole transport system including the motorway programme, the improvement of classified roads and the sanction of nearby development. The Ministry of Power route the high voltage national system of current distribution, and locate generating stations. This list would be incomplete without reference to the considerable powers for land planning held by the Nationalized Boards which own land such as the Transport Commission, the Nature Conservancy and the National Parks Commission.

Transport, industrial location, power, public utilities and the use of agricultural land must be key elements in any comprehensive approach to national planning problems—yet their sanction is not the direct responsibility of the planning ministry. Fundamental surveys require to be undertaken if the planning relationships which exist between these problems are to provide a basis for decisive action. 'By various agencies, the landscape of Britain is being rapidly transformed. New power stations . . . are under construction; a new system of highways is taking shape; certain railways are under electrification; new coal-mines are being sunk—others closed; new oil refineries appear; new steel works are planned. . . . All the developments are certain to affect in varying ways the economic and social life of the regions in which they are sited or through which they pass. Yet it is apparent that the schemes are conceived by different ministries, nationalized corporations and other organizations, in isolation from one another and with little thought to their bearing upon the regional economic geography of the country.'[6]

The urgent need for an integrated approach was recognized in each of the wartime planning reports, but these recommendations were not embodied in subsequent legislation. Informed criticisms, as above, have resulted. Politically, both the Conservative Bow Group and Socialist Commentary have emphasized the necessity for more positive and energetic government action, and planning arguments for a more constructive approach are frequent.[7] One great function of planning research in this pressure towards change is to record and to understand those problems which exist at the present and, in particular, to portray the snowball of land-use consequences which result from a major development decision such as the provision of a new highway.

The planning functions of local government

The need for competent surveys and research is equally as great at the more intimate local levels of public administration. Planning powers have been delegated by parliament to the Administrative Counties and the County Boroughs. Joint Boards, representing the interests of more than one administrative authority, may be responsible for the areas of National Parks. These planning authorities are staffed by local government officers, in contrast with the civil servants of the national ministries. Borderline between these two administrative categories are the New Town Development Corporations, charged with the duty of creating new and living environments.

All planning authorities perform three major tasks.[8] They are required by law to prepare a plan indicating the manner of the proposed and anticipated development, and the stages by which it is expected to be carried out; this plan, which includes statutory maps and a written statement of proposals and policies, defines sites for development, allocates areas of land for defined purposes, and designates land as subject to compulsory purchase; the plan is generally for a period of 20 years and is reviewed regularly at periods of not more than every five years. In order to implement the plan, authorities may acquire land, attract resources, phase development and themselves develop or sponsor the development of land. To make sure that all development accords with the planning policy for the area, the plans of proposed development must be submitted to the local planning authority and these proposals can either be approved unconditionally, approved subject to certain decisions, or be refused; the final arbiter between an aggrieved applicant and a planning authority is the minister, who may hold a public local inquiry. 'A planning authority may wish to guide, divert, influence, modify, alter, suppress or stimulate development. And it will wish to do so not so much to make the development conform to a plan but rather in order to pursue its land planning objectives. . . . When a planning authority is weighing up the advantages and disadvantages of incorporating into its plan a particular development programme or proposal, or one in a particular form, or considering a development application, its outlook is not that of the developer. Its horizon of interest is wider and its objectives are different. It must hold the balance between all developers, and between them and the local and national interest.'[9]

This careful and considered approach to planning demands a substantial volume of survey information, including the continuous collection and interpretation of all appropriate statistical data, the organization of special surveys to understand the implications of problems such as slum clearance or the pressure for central area office accommodation, and special studies for the purpose of effective development control. In addition there is the detailed work on which to formulate planning objectives, and to provide a sound analytical basis for the development plan, its quinquennial review and redevelopment projects. A large administrative county may employ perhaps ten qualified staff, mainly graduates in geography, in their research section. In the smaller boroughs and counties surveys may be undertaken by persons with a general planning qualification rather than with a specific training in one of the research disciplines. Outside consultants may be retained for the more difficult investigations. It must, however, be admitted with chagrin that several important British cities have no trained research workers on their staff, and basic surveys of the type suggested below have not been undertaken.

There remains abundant scope for the research worker, slowly through the quality and practical nature of his various studies, to influence a more realistic approach to the problems of planning than is now apparent. This, in essence, is what many exponents of survey analysis have been doing since the Town and Country Planning Act of 1947 became operative. They have faced in many instances, though not always, opposition from the established professional interests of architects, engineers and surveyors. But, in the other direction, sociologists, geographers and economists have not contributed as much to planning thought as might have been anticipated from the enthusiasm of the immediate post-war years. Where, for example, are the detailed post-1950 British studies of population movements, industrial location, patterns of urban growth, declining towns, expanding areas, redevelopment projects, new towns and so on? Some worth-while studies exist; much more work remains to be done.

The circle is a vicious one in that certain authorities deny or pay only lip service to the need for research, yet only through valid analytical surveys can it be shown that efficient and beneficial planning will reduce costs. Research may also be regarded as 'inconvenient' or 'unpopular' to local government, because its findings, emerging from systematic and unbiassed surveys, need not be in accordance with established ideas, current policy or that which is politically expedient. 'If the experience of the past seven years has demonstrated one thing more than another, it is our woeful ignorance of essential facts . . . once legislation is passed, administrators do not welcome disturbing new facts. So the conscientious and painstaking civil servant (or local government officer—author's addition) working from the book in the office may well make an increasing number of wrong decisions.'[10]

A further difficulty in conducting valid local surveys is the absence of a regional approach as existed with the joint advisory committees of the 1930's. The County Boroughs are divorced from their city-regions, a conurbation can be divided between several planning authorities and the Administrative Counties must be planned without direct control over the development activities of the County Boroughs. The Lancashire plan, for example, excludes Manchester, Rochdale, Bolton, Blackpool and other major centres in the county from its jurisdiction. Land provisions are made to meet the extra-territorial requirements of these excluded localities, but the scope of planning surveys is diminished by the administrative arrangements. Problems such as the siting of industry, arrangements for the dispersal and reception of an overspill population, green belts, the total demand for houses, the shifting pattern of employment across a coalfield area, the organization of comprehensive 'origin and destination' traffic surveys, and so on, all demand a regional approach to the content of the planning surveys and the formulation of definitive policy. No machinery now exists for a complete coverage of information on these subjects, though the Ministry of Housing and Local Government have powers to create regional planning boards and the reform of local government may usher in a single planning authority over conurbations.[11]

The lamp of Geddes

The logical but not necessarily the political approach to land-use problems involves five consecutive and interwoven stages of a continuous planning process—survey, projection, policy, implementation and assessment.

Patrick Geddes pioneered this systematic approach to planning, and his arguments epitomize the need for positive surveys. 'As our surveys advance we become at home in our region, throughout its time and its space up to the present day. From thence the past and the present cannot but open out into the possible. For our survey of things as they are—that is as they have become—must ever suggest ideas as to their further becoming—their further possibilities. In this way our surveys are seen to have a practical interest beyond their purely scientific interest. In a word, the survey prepares for and points towards the Plan. . . . Such surveys must always be dispassionately scientific. Our endeavour first and foremost to "see the thing as it is", and next to co-ordinate it with other things, until we reach a mental picture of each of our regions and communities in all the elaborations of their place, work and people, throughout the past and in their present, in all of which good and evil are strangely intermingled. Our science thus cannot but point to action, our diagnosis to treatment.'[12]

These philosophies have become accepted tenets of British

planning policy. The principal enabling act, the Town and Country Planning Act, 1947, stated categorically that 'every local planning authority shall carry out a survey together with a plan'.[13] Planning surveys have been made obligatory rather than permissive by legislation, and proposals involving the use and development of land must now be formulated from the basis of established facts. If planning decisions are to result from an intelligent appreciation of the problem, and if objectives are to take fully into account the complexity of the various factors involved, then the assessment must be based on understanding rather than supposition. Forethought has become more impoitant to realistic planning than personal prejudice or preconceived ideas.

A survey does not just start of its own accord; it has to be organized with meticulous care from beginning to end. The various processes concerned with the collection, the processing and the interpretation of data must be undertaken objectively, honestly, with integrity and without bias. The attitude must be to examine a particular concept or to investigate a problem in detail. The researcher will rarely know what conclusions will emerge from his surveys; his métier is the unrestricted study of evidence and his first allegiance is to the quality of this material. Studies must be impartial: the task is neither to prove that a particular policy is correct, nor to suggest that a particular objective would be desirable; this may emerge from the studies, but the end must never be permitted to prejudice the careful and methodical approach to data. The concern is always with the scientific method of investigation, and it is this factor which provides the essential ingredient of a purposeful planning survey. 'The man who classifies fact of any kind whatever, who sees their mutual relation and describes the sequences, is applying the scientific method. It is not the facts themselves which make science but the method by which they are dealt with.'[14]

The first stage in this methodical approach is to state precisely the questions which are to be answered by the survey. This requires the clear formulation of survey objectives, an explicit statement of the problem in meaningful terms and the rigorous exclusion of subjects marginal to the central theme of the investigation. The more closely the subject-matter can be defined, the greater the detail in which the characteristics of a given situation may be observed, and the greater the usefulness of the final report. It is usually impracticable to incorporate additional terms of reference at a late stage in the inquiry, and any consequential changes in coverage will waste time and incur unnecessary expense. Every part of the survey must be thought out beforehand. Exploratory studies and pilot surveys should be used to test the validity of the method of approach and to suggest amendments to the chosen techniques.

When the questions to be covered have been settled the methods to be used in collecting the information must be determined. What information can be obtained from the mapping of field data, by observation, from questionnaires, by interview and by the study of existing sources? What do the statistics cover? Which method of survey, or combination of methods, can be expected to yield the most effective results? Is a sample survey justified and, if so, which technique would be the most reliable in the circumstances? What size of sample is appropriate for the requisite accuracy and with the available resources of time and money? Are the resources of the office sufficient in number and kind, or is outside assistance necessary? What staff are needed, and of what background and training? Can the costs be assessed in terms of salaries and wages, the expense of meetings, the cost of equipment, the printing of forms, travel expenses and the cost of publications? Are grants or other forms of income available? When will the field-work be undertaken, and what outside consultation is necessary? What will be the length of the investigation?

In answering these apparently simple but in reality complex questions of procedure, personal experience is important. Textbooks on method, descriptions of statistical tabulations, bibliographies of published sources and accounts of previous surveys in the same field all provide much useful information, but never replace the practical knowledge to be gained by direct study. Data must be handled before its complexities can be wholly appreciated; there can be no complete substitute for the reality of personal experience in survey. This, in its turn, provides the researcher with the satisfaction of tackling and resolving a problem. Like C. P. Snow's character, Arthur Miles, 'one can do science because one enjoys . . . the problem solving process'.

Or again, 'I believe that social research is not only a full-scale intellectual exercise but also a personal experience, and a very satisfying personal experience, if it comes to that. The sociologists often speak about the impact of interviewers or respondents, but the impact is mutual.'[15]

No amount of subsequent manipulation or refinements in statistical analysis can overcome deficiencies which are introduced during the initial stages in the collection of the basic data. Any inaccuracies or bias are passed onwards to the later stages of the research process, and each stage of the investigation relies inexorably on the competence of the preliminary survey work. It is a truism that the quality of the final product can never be better than the quality of its component materials. Examples of such basic studies would include surveys of industrial location, land-use patterns, traffic generation, population growth, economic vitality or the functions of towns in a region.

The subsequent stages of planning thought should also involve the research worker. Survey data must be projected forward into the future. To what extent can future needs be foreseen from present characteristics and current trends? What population can be anticipated in 'x' years' time? What are the implications of this future total population, and of its age and sex structure, on land needs? What population will have to be rehoused over the period of the development plan? What school provision and community needs are required? What volumes of traffic can be expected? Again our inspiration may be Geddes. 'It is surely of the very essence of the evolution concept—hard though it be to realize it, more difficult still to apply it—that it should not only inquire how this of today may have come out of that of yesterday, but be foreseeing and preparing for what the morrow is even now in its turn bringing towards birth . . . the main problem [is] that of the discernment of present tendency, amid the apparent phantasmagoria of change.'[16]

The stage of policy formulation and the design of planning proposals will seek to resolve the problems posed by the survey and its projection into the future. What are the space requirements of this particular need? How will the necessary land be allocated? Which sites should prove most suitable? How might the development best be integrated into the existing pattern of communities? What will be the relationship between buildings and public open spaces? How will traffic circulate? What are the probable repercussions of the proposed development, and what further proposals are necessary to meet these foreseeable contingencies? The research worker should be expected to contribute on these aspects together with the relationships between different building uses, the demand for space, the probable generation of traffic and other factors which require determination by careful investigation.

The purpose of this thought is to achieve the construction of a desired scheme, whether it be the best siting of industrial development, a motorway, afforestation, a residential estate, a new town or the retention of land under intensive arable production. This stage of implementation may involve the legal machinery to acquire land; the attraction of the requisite finance, services, facilities and building labour to create the sponsored development; the co-ordination and careful phasing of the various parts envisaged in the programme; the preparation of detailed drawings, the letting of contracts and the disposal of the completed buildings as contributory elements towards the creation of a new habitat or environment. The function of the research worker is to keep continually under review the assumptions and goals on which the plan was based. Do the survey findings, projections and recommendations remain relevant? What new events have changed the situation? Has the development of land proceeded as anticipated? What re-surveys or further surveys should be undertaken?

The final assessment is then the crucial examination of the completed development including the critical appreciation of standards and the use made of the buildings and public open spaces. The implementation of a scheme should usher in a whole series of relevant investigations. The content of these further studies would examine critically the degree of success of the project, state the extent to which the objects of the scheme have been realized, expose the deficiencies and advantages of the development, examine whether assumptions have materialized and generally deduce the lessons of practical experience for the future benefit of both the planners and the planned. There must be continuous amendments to planning techniques, programmes and proposals in the light of current knowledge and the changing pattern of demands. Neither plans nor policies can ever attain finality.

Survey, the collection of relevant facts, and research, the analysis and interpretation of this data and its application to planning problems, are thus important aspects of the subject throughout the whole of the planning process. These investigations by themselves are not planning; nor can these various studies be regarded as of more importance than the legal, engineering, architectural, landscape, administrative or other facets of town and country planning. 'The researcher is neither an information-giver, except as a voluntary act of charity, nor an oracle reader. He functions in his own right, and just as much as and no more than the professional planner, to make a distinctive contribution to the total complex which is purposeful planning. . . . The acquisition of relevant knowledge and the orderly presentation of information in survey form is but the starting point of the research activity.'[17]

Planning involves team-work, and in this the research worker has a significant contribution to make. Surveys, narrowly conceived, initiate the processes of planning thought; in the reality of practice they have much to contribute at all stages of planning.

The training of the research worker

Many graduates in geography have entered the planning profession. Of the technical staff in county planning departments in 1961, 17·1 per cent held university degrees and, of these, 9·4 per cent were geographers.[18] T. W. Freeman introduces his book with the categoric statement that 'planning has an inescapable geographical basis. . . . It is essential to the planner's work, for the planner must understand the existing landscape before he tries to reform it, both in town and country.'[19] Or again, in the words of Professor Stamp, 'the past fifty years·have been spent in developing geographical methods of survey and analysis. . . . The time has surely come when those same methods . . . can be used in helping towards the solution of some of the great world problems—the increasing pressure of population on space, the development of under-developed areas, or the attempt to improve living conditions, which is the object of town and country planning. Such is, indeed, the field of applied geography.'[20]

But geography is not planning, despite the mutual concern of both disciplines with the use of land and with the complex of relationships which are involved. A geographical survey need not forecast future trends, nor need it make recommendations on future policy. The geographer may lack the creative imagination required of the planner, or his training may have emphasized certain facets of the subject to the exclusion of the broad synoptic view. Other forms of disciplined training in method, e.g. geology, economics, statistics and sociology, have contributed towards planning surveys in both the Civil Service and in Local Government. Further, many planning surveys require more training than is normally available to either the geographer, economist or sociologist; an appreciation of the age or the condition of buildings demands an understanding of structure, construction and materials; an assessment of mining subsidence requires the acumen of an engineer; the possibilities of reclaiming derelict land merits the knowledge of a soil scientist, botanist or landscape architect; and analysis of traffic flow and movement will involve the traffic engineer. The research team must be able to undertake social, economic and geographic surveys, and be able to apply their various techniques in the elucidation of many current problems. A synoptic grasp is needed rather than specialism.

The student interested in planning, whether an undergraduate or leaving school, can attend one of the recognized schools of planning. Manchester University, for example, offers a four-year full-time degree course in town and country planning, a three-year part-time evening course for graduates and for persons with certain other professional qualifications, and a two-year (one year full-time and one year part-time) post-graduate course. These courses provide exemption from the examinations of the Town Planning Institute, the professional body concerned generally with the advancement of planning and of the planning profession.[21]

Although instruction in survey methods and techniques is provided by all planning schools, it is to be regretted that no educational establishment is concerned primarily with the task of advancing planning surveys and research as such. Nor is there yet any national or centralized research unit devoted to the study of planning problems, techniques, objectives and standards. The need for such an institute should already be apparent from the nature of the land-use problems to which planning seeks to contribute. Many empirical processes are concerned with redevelopment in outmoded urban environments, the dispersal of people to new or expanded towns, the creation of Green belts, the location of industry and the movement of urban traffic. As planning becomes a more positive tool for the use and development of land, so too does basic research gain in significance.

A research unit could sponsor detailed investigations in association with and into topics suggested by local Planning authorities and government departments, and evaluate the evidence for the greater understanding of the problems involved. The knowledge thus gained would be disseminated by publications, conferences and through the interchange of staff to secure its application in practice. New techniques and methods of approach would be continually under scrutiny in an attempt to improve and to refine existing methods. These activities could be in association with the training of graduate research workers by the best of all possible means—learning through the medium of practical experience in live projects.

These ideas are not new. A national institution for the advancement of planning was advocated by the Schuster Committee. 'Liaison through publications and periodical conferences should be established, so that the importance of individual pieces of work could be assessed, results discussed, standards evolved and new methods brought to the notice of all workers in this field. With this object in view . . . there is need for a national institution to watch the whole field of relevant study and research and promote liaison between those working in different ways in this field.'[22] The authoritative voice of the Royal Commission on Local Government in Greater London stated 'there is an urgent need for the existence of a body which will conduct continuous research and provide continuously to the planning authority the necessary material on which intelligent guesses as to future trends and the possibility of controlling them and directing them can be based. Nothing of the kind exists at the present time.'[23]

The research institute could be associated with a university, preferably one with a planning school and with a tradition for social and economic investigation, or might operate within the framework of an existing research organization such as the Department of Scientific and Industrial Research, or could be an independent research body such as the Medical Research Council. The importance of planning as a formative force in moulding the British landscape and environment merits a foundation of this calibre, and substantial national contributions towards its financial costs.[24]

Conclusion

Town and country planning has neither precise boundaries nor rigidly defined terms of reference, but has nevertheless become a significant controlling force in Great Britain and elsewhere for a number of compelling reasons. 'Planning should be dynamic and exciting . . . it should be intelligible . . . it should be continuously debated when elected representatives and other groups meet. Planning comprises a series of related decisions which should give a sense of direction as well as objectives. It must also give tangible and meaningful shape to all building activities. It must encourage economic and social efficiency and, in so doing, give delight.'[25] Geographers and architects, economists and engineers, sociologists and administrators, laymen and civil servants, the general public and members of Parliament must each make significant contributions. The role of survey is to study the situation factually and objectively, to present clear and carefully reasoned reports, to provide the necessary understanding before decisions for development are made and to evaluate the effects of development.

The research worker, through valid surveys, must establish the results of the present inadequate approach to the problems of land use. He must continually be examining, analysing, criticizing and seeking to suggest improvements to current policies. This was the inspiring method of pioneers such as Frederic Le Play, Charles Booth, Patrick Geddes, Professor Bowley and of other reformers who helped to develop the scientific spirit and methods of social investigation. The approach remains relevant to the conditions of today. One function of the planning survey, as stressed by Patrick Geddes, is to inspire action: 'Our surveys thus cannot but point to action, our diagnosis to treatment. With a fuller knowledge than before, social actions will tend to be more sure and more skilful'.[26] The training of planning research workers and the creation of a national research institute for the study of land-use problems would contribute towards this end.

1   F. S. Chapin, *Urban Land Use Planning*, 1957, pp. xiii–xiv. The most important single British source is L. Keeble, *Principles and Practice of Town and Country Planning*, Estates Gazette, 1959. F. B. Gillie and P. L. Hughes, *Some Principles of Land Planning*, 1950; B. J. Collins, *Development Plans Explained*, H.M.S.O., 1952; and P. Self, *Cities in Flood*, 1957, provide admirable introductions to the scope and problems of British planning. See also articles in the *Journal of the Town Planning Institute, Town Planning Review, Planning Outlook* and *Town and Country Planning*.

2   *The Control of Land Use*, Cmd 6537, 1944, p. 1. (The italics are the author's.)

3   See, for example, C. Abrams in 'Urban Land Problems and Policies', *Housing and Town and Country Planning Bulletin* 7, United Nations, 5T/SOA/SER.C/7, 1953, pp. 1–58. Also C. M. Haar, *Land Use Planning: a Casebook on the Use, Misuse and Re-Use of Urban Land*, 1959.   .

4   *Final Report of the Expert Committee on Compensation and Betterment*, Cmd 6386, 1942, paras. 360–2. The other reports are *Report of the Royal Commission on the Distribution of the Industrial Population*, Cmd 6153, 1940, and *Report of the Committee on Land Utilization in Rural Areas*, Cmd 6378, 1942.

5   Minister of Town and Country Planning Act, 1943, section I; Central Office of Information, *Town and Country Planning in Great Britain*, 1959; and the sequence of *Annual Reports* describe the range of responsibilities. Ministry of Housing and Local Government, Sectional List, H.M.S.O., contains a complete list of government publications.

6   M. J. Wise, *Industrial Location: a Geographical Approach*, 1959, pp. 33–5.

7   Bow Group, *Let our Cities Live*, 1960; 'The Face of Britain: a Policy for Town and Country Planning', *Socialist Commentary*, 1961; 'Land Use in an Urban Environment: A General View of Town and Country Planning', *Town Planning Review*, vol. XXXII, 1961.

SURVEYS AND THE PLANNING PROCESS   29

8 See B. J. Collins, *Development Plans Explained*, H.M.S.O., 1951; D. Heap, *An Outline of Planning Law*, 1960.

9 N. Lichfield, *Economics of Planned Development*, Estates Gazette, 1956, p. 35.

10 L. D. Stamp, quoted in P.E.P., *The Approach to Land Use Planning*, vol. XVIII, no. 329, 1951, p.17.

11 Town and Country Planning Act, 1947, section 4. See *Royal Commission on Local Government in Greater London, 1957–1960*, Cmd 1164, 1960, pp. 200–3.

12 Patrick Geddes, *Cities in Evolution*, 1949, pp. xxvi–xxvii.

13 Town and Country Planning Act, 1947, section 5(1).

14 K. Pearson, *The Grammar of Science*, 1911, pp. 10–12.

15 F. Zweig, *The British Worker*, 1952, p.17.

16 Geddes, op. cit., 1949, pp. 1–2.

17 F. J. McCulloch, 'Research and Planning', *Town Planning Review*, vol. XXIII, 1952, pp. 33–4.

18 *Journal of the Town Planning Institute*, vol. XLVII, 1961, pp. 140–1.

19 T. W. Freeman, *Geography and Planning*, 1958, p.13.

20 L. Dudley Stamp, *Applied Geography*, 1960, p.10.

21 A list of approved university and other planning courses may be obtained from the Secretary, 18 Ashley Place, London, S.W.1.

22 *Report of the Committee on Qualifications of Planners*, Cmd 8059, 1950, p. 64.

23 Cmd 1164, op. cit., para 350.

24 Canadian action offers some lessons for Britain. A Committee of Inquiry sponsored by the Royal Architectural Institute of Canada reported on the 'Design of the Residential Environment' in 1960 (*R.A.I.C. Journal*, May 1960). Its recommendations for action included the need for a permanent Canadian Institute of Urban Studies. A Founding Conference of the 'Canadian Council of Urban and Regional Research' was held in March 1962 with representatives from universities, municipal governments, federal and provincial governments, and private enterprise. The Council was formally established in April 1962 with financial assistance from the Government of Canada and the Ford Foundation. Its objectives are to encourage and promote urban and regional research. Details may be obtained from Canadian Council on Urban and Regional Research, 56 Sparks Street, Ottawa, Canada.

25 G. Stephenson, *Planning*, an address to the National Housing and Planning Conference, 1952.

26 Geddes, op. cit., p. xxvii.

2
SOURCES OF INFORMATION

As a prelude to most surveys and throughout the investigation, the research worker should be conversant with the availability and usefulness of all appropriate sources of reference and of information. These include books, papers in professional journals, directories, maps, documents, and statistical records, official and unofficial, published and unpublished. This chapter will be concerned with two vital elements in this methodical approach to survey—the use of the library and its resources, and statistical sources of information.

The library and its resources

The research worker must be able to use a library intelligently and to take full advantage of its varied resources.[1] A thorough study of the literature in the proposed field will enable the research worker to appreciate the usefulness of different survey techniques from previous studies, indicate those aspects of the topic which might require special investigation, permit the comparison of local findings with the evidence from elsewhere and assist in his statement and definition of objectives. Indeed, the whole of pertinent planning studies can be developed around the material available in library collections. Thus demographic trends may be assessed from published statistics, an essay on industrial location could emerge from an appraisal of trade directories and earlier studies can be summarized and evaluated so that further research may concentrate on the relevant aspects of a problem. More frequently, a library is used in conjunction with field studies and with other methods of obtaining information.

The success of research work within a library begins with an understanding of the classification system. Catalogues are usually by name (mainly author, but sometimes editor or translator) and by subject in Dewey Decimal or other order, but may also be by title. Card catalogues should be studied under every variety of possible headings because information on a place can be under town, county, regional or national headings, and subjects may be either specific or under a range of generic expressions. The principal limitations of the card catalogues are that they exclude literature in periodicals and refer only to sources of information within the library; they do not pretend to be comprehensive on a particular subject and, in research, it is often necessary to use the resources of more than one library.

An indication of the material available in the major British libraries may be regarded as a fundamental source to further information on a particular subject. The British Museum, which receives all works published in Britain, has published a *General Catalogue of Printed Books* containing a list of all books published up to 1955. Another useful compendium is the index to the British Library of Political and Economic Science, *A London Bibliography of the Social Sciences*. The annual volumes published by the Council of the British National Bibliography, *British National Bibliography*, list every new work published in Great Britain, and similar works are available for most other countries. For further source material the four volumes of T. Besterman, *A world bibliography of bibliographies, and of bibliographical catalogues, indexes, and the like*, 1955–6, may be consulted.

Periodical articles represent a source of increasing importance. Many journals prepare annual indexes, but their consultation for a number of different journals and over a period of time is cumbersome. To overcome this problem the Library Association publish annually *The Subject Index to Periodicals*, which contains an author index as from 1961, and regional lists were introduced in 1954. *Sociological Abstracts* (ed. L. P. Chall) and the H. Wilson Company's *International Index: a Guide to Periodical Literature in the Social Sciences and Humanities* are both published quarterly in New York. Each of these periodical indexes provides an extremely valuable indication of further source material, though their coverage of journals is selective, which restricts their usefulness. Thus the

British Journal of Sociology and the *Sociological Review* are included in all three indexes; *Planning Outlook*, *Town and Country Planning*, *Town Planning Review* and *The Times Review of Industry* are included only in the index of the Library Association; the *Journal of the Town Planning Institute* is not included in any of the three indexes. The periodical indexes are not as comprehensive as their titles might suggest.

The only British daily morning newspaper to maintain an index is *The Times*, which publishes one every two months. The files of local newspapers are not usually available for inspection, and a time-consuming search for information through previous issues in the local reference library is normally the only method which can be adopted for local information.

With regard to specific planning sources of information, the most comprehensive is the catalogue for the library of the Ministry of Housing and Local Government. An *Index to Periodical Articles*, prepared every two months for internal departmental circulation, is based on the 300 periodicals received in this library. A *Classified Accessions List* of new books and reports catalogued into the library is also prepared. Copies of these valuable indices are held in the library of the Town Planning Institute, but are not otherwise generally available. A wider distribution, possibly in the form of supplements to the *Journal of the Town Planning Institute*, would be welcomed, as would the publication of the catalogue of the libraries in the Ministry of Housing and Local Government and in the Town Planning Institute.

A useful record of British Planning Research between 1948 and 1958 has been compiled by the Town Planning Institute.[2] This book catalogues the details of papers and books submitted by research workers, but does not refer to other publications and published reports on the same subject. This gargantuan task has yet to be attempted, and would provide an important initial function for the proposed National Institute of Planning Research. In addition, the *News Sheet of the International Federation for Housing and Planning* and *Ekistics*, published in The Hague and Athens respectively, include digests of published articles. The U.N.E.S.C.O. volumes on the Social Sciences, *Directory of Current Periodical Abstracts and*

Bibliographies (ed. T. Besterman), contain many useful references, as also do the various volumes published by U.N.E.S.C.O. in the series *Current Sociology: a trend report and bibliography.* The *Journal of the American Institute of Planners* has a cumulative and annotated index, 1925–58. (See p. 60 for other American sources.)

Many books and papers contain lists of references to further source material as an introduction to the consecutive snowball process of assimilation. If consulted methodically and in conjunction with all the above sources of information, then the researcher should be introduced to most of the available information on his subject. It is never possible to guarantee that every source has been consulted. The problems of keeping abreast with current knowledge and thought in a new discipline are particularly difficult. The urgent need for a central research institute in planning to act as a central bureau with access to all planning literature and reports, and for the wide circulation of information to the profession, would seem to be essential if planning is to advance in its status and in the public performance of its professional duties.

Librarians are invariably helpful when approached with a genuine request for assistance. They would, however, be the first to emphasize that their function is to guide the reader to sources of information; it is not the librarian's responsibility to assess the reliability or the usefulness of data. Not all published sources are either accurate or trustworthy; spurious literature is not unknown. An author may be careless, biassed or incompetent, in whole or in part; primary sources may have been misquoted or misinterpreted; the method of approach may have led to untrustworthy conclusions. The research worker must develop a critical attitude towards all sources of information, including his own findings, and evaluate carefully the worth of every source that is being consulted. A library neither endorses the reliability of its material nor pretends to be infallible in its coverage.

The use of available statistics

The research worker must handle statistics, yet the available facts on a particular subject are scattered over a wide variety of sources, and the information changes from time to time to affect their use and meaning. A *Guide to Official Statistics* flourished from 1922 to 1938 and indexed all statistics in government publications, but has not been reissued post-war. No comprehensive or continuous list now exists either on the availability of material or the accuracy of data, though several miscellaneous sources are available.[3] The ensuing comments will therefore suggest the principal sources of information which were available at March 1961, and the difficulties which must be appreciated before the statistics can be understood and applied to the solution of current planning problems. Incorrect deductions are all too easy and must be avoided.

The majority of published statistics have been collected by official sources. Some result from the administrative responsibilities of a government department; others have been obtained from a specific enquiry. The former category would include data from the Board of Trade about the volume of approved industrial development, and Ministry of Labour statistics on the level of employment; examples of specific inquiries include the decennial Census of Population and statistical series such as the Registrar General's *Annual Statistical Review*. Statistics obtained for administrative purposes tend to be more difficult to analyse objectively because their correct interpretation depends on some knowledge of departmental procedures; internal changes may affect the continuity of a series, and statutory regulations will influence the coverage of data. The statistics result as a by-product of administrative convenience, and their use is subject to this major determinant of their character and quality. With the more specific studies, the methods of collection are usually known and definitions are published but, even so, the continuity of a series may be difficult to interpret.

A fact by itself is of limited importance. It gains in significance when comparisons can be made either in time or with conditions elsewhere, but outwardly comparable data may differ in its composition. A boundary can have been changed, a definition revised in its meaning, the coverage of data may have altered or the dates of collection may not be comparable. The research worker must anticipate these possibilities and examine the notes of tables for possible variations in the coverage of data. It is helpful to work backwards in time in historical investigations. Changes can be referred to only in subsequent volumes, and revised figures for previous dates on the basis of the new definition or boundary may be included in the later reports.

Statistics are often collected in confidence or with the promise of anonymity to the donor. A strong moral obligation exists not to disclose individual details, even to bonafide investigators, and no research worker would wish to destroy the confidence of those who have provided his working information. For government statistics, where the provision of information may result from legal enactment, the Statistics of Trade Act 1947 reinforces this accepted practice of research workers. 'No individual estimates or returns, and no information relating to an individual undertaking shall . . . be disclosed.' Further, any report or summary must be so arranged 'as to prevent any particulars published therein from being identified as being particulars relating to any individual person or undertaking'.[4] Official practice will never take a risk on these issues. As a result, basic information which could be analysed and presented by the research worker without disclosing individual identities, cannot be used. For example, a study of evidence within the Board of Trade on the movement of industry, desirable in order to assess the effectiveness of national policy towards industrial location, could not be countenanced. The direct employment returns of the Ministry of Labour, giving the number of persons employed in each establishment, are confidential yet may be vital for the formulation of local land-planning objectives.

The time-lag between the collection of information and its publication is a subject of some importance. Obviously some delay is inevitable, but could not some of the more important local statistics be made available sooner? The mid-June employment information is available for Exchange areas next February or March; the 'Usual Residence and Workplace' and the 'Occupation' volumes of the 1951 Census of Population were published in 1956, and the 'Industry Tables' appeared in 1957. Happily, the information in the 1961 census may appear sooner than its predecessors through the use of a computer. The first provisional report was published in two months and all the detailed tabulations are expected to be complete within three years, which is less than half the time taken to bring out the reports on the 1951 census. (See note on p. 84.)

The collection of government statistics is not centralized in any one bureau but is essentially on a departmental basis. Some general responsibility for the co-ordination of statistics is however exercised by the Central Statistical Office which, as a part of its duties, prepares the *Monthly Digest of Statistics* and the *Annual Abstract of Statistics* on the basis of information from a variety of different government departments and its own investigations. To facilitate this function of 'the collection from departments of a regular series of figures on a coherent and well-ordered basis', the Central Statistical Office has prepared uniform systems of classification such as the *Standard Industrial Classification* and the *Occupational Classification*.

Population statistics

The most important single source of information is the Census of Population, taken decennially since 1801 with the one exception of 1941.[5] Since 1841 its details have been based on the schedule completed by the head of the household. The principal questions asked in 1951 included sex, age, relationship to the head of the household, marital status, birthplace, nationality, occupation, industry, place of usual residence, place of work, fertility of married women, number of living-rooms, possession of household amenities and the terminal age of full-time education. New questions introduced for the first time in 1961 include the qualifications of scientists and technologists, whether dwellings are rented or owned, length of residence at the census address and, if for less than one year, place of residence a year ago. Quite apart from the published details, certain census statistics may be obtained from the Registrar General at an additional cost for enumeration districts, areas with about 250 households for which one census enumerator is responsible. This facility should be particularly welcome for areas of change, such as redevelopment sites, new housing estates and localities receiving an overspill population.

The census population at 1951 was the *de facto* population, otherwise called the 'enumerated' or the 'census' population. This comprised 'all persons enumerated on land, in barges and boats on inland waters, in all vessels in ports and at anchorages at census midnight other than ships of foreign navies, and all persons in boats on fishing or coastwise voyages which returned to port during the census month not having proceeded from a port outside Great Britain'. Many of the census details, such as age, sex and marital status, are related to this definition which is the actual number of people present in an area on a given date. It includes visitors from abroad and elsewhere in the United Kingdom, residents at home— but not those normally resident in the area but away on census night —and the crews and passengers of ships. It excludes members of the armed forces and the merchant navy away from the country between 9 April and 1 May; their families, if resident, would be included. Children at boarding school and students in college would normally be on vacation, and would tend to be included in their home area; likewise the seasonal population would be excluded from holiday resorts as the count was in the slack period of April. (As the 1921 census was taken in June, comparisons in holiday, school and university areas may be invalid.) It is interesting that, whereas U.K. armed forces stationed abroad were excluded, U.S. forces stationed here were included.

    Inter-censal estimates by contrast are of the 'home' population, known either as the *de jure* population or the population normally resident in an area. The available information refers to 30 June of each year and is published at the end of December in the General Register Office *Annual Estimates of the Population of England and Wales and of Local Authority Areas*. The data are later incorporated in the *Annual Statistical Review*, together with the number of births and deaths over the calendar year. This concept of the 'home' population includes members of the armed forces stationed in the area; undergraduates, pupils in boarding schools and patients in psychiatric hospitals have been treated generally as part of the population of the area; patients in general hospitals and convalescent homes have generally been included under the area of their home residence.

    The 'home' population minus the armed forces becomes the

'civilian' population. The mid-year estimates of population supplied confidentially to local planning authorities by the Ministry of Housing and Local Government suggest the size of the 'civilian' population. As a great reliance is placed upon population statistics in planning surveys and policy, it is imperative to state clearly whether the data refer to the 'census', 'home' or the 'civilian' populations. These different 'populations' are not usually comparable, and the implications of the three definitions must be understood before their salient characteristics and trends can be interpreted. The civilian population is particularly relevant for most planning purposes, including the projection of population.

The total population of wards and of parishes (N.B. not villages) is given in the county volumes of the 1951 census. For calculating the population within smaller areas a house-to-house survey yields the most useful data as other facts (e.g. household size, age and sex structure, numbers in employment and their place of work) can be obtained at the same time. For general estimates the electoral roll, to be discussed in Chapter 3 as a sampling frame, may be used. The number of voters—those aged 21 and over—in each unit area is known, as is their total in the town; the ratio of the total number of voters to the total civilian population in private households is applied to the number of electors in each unit area to provide an estimate of the local population. The proportion of non-voters may not be the same in each area as in the ward, and sample surveys need to be undertaken to check whether adjustments are desirable for varying ratios of children to adult, for married heads of households under voting age, for emigration or immigration since the preparation of the electoral roll, or to allow for a non-voting element because of nationality. Calculations based on the electoral roll provide a broad indication of population distribution by small areas, and may be used for the analysis of population trends within an urban area. The resultant details are estimates rather than precise figures, and refer to the civilian population.

A key element in planning is the assessment of future population size. If the age-sex structure of the population is known, then the population in 10 years' time will be the population in each age group less the anticipated number of deaths. The survivors of the present population aged 0–4 will be 10–14, and so on. Most of the future population are alive now, and the number of years' births to be added on at the base of the population pyramid will depend on the length of the forecast. No forecast expects to be precise, and must depend on assumptions about trends in mortality and fertility. The shorter the term of the forecast, the greater the probable accuracy, because the present trends and conditions are known and births over the next 15 years will be to the existing female population aged 0–29.

National projections on this basis by sex and age for 5, 10, 15, 20, 30 and 40 years hence are published in the December *Quarterly Return for England and Wales*. The more significant projections for local authority districts have been undertaken by the Registrar General, and are supplied to local planning authorities by the Ministry of Housing and Local Government.[5] The first provisional projections were based on the mid-1947 population estimates, and were calculated for mid-1962. These were succeeded in 1949 when the *Estimates of the Sex and Age Distribution of the Civilian Population at 31st December, 1947*, provided a more reliable base for the projection. These revised projections were to December 1962 and separate figures were given for children aged 0–4, 5–9 and 10–14, for males and females of working age, and for males and females of retirement age and over. A projection to 1971 in total only was also supplied, and this projection is of particular historic importance as it was used by most planning authorities in the preparation of their first (i.e. 1951) development plans. Subsequently, new projections to 1971 have been prepared on the basis of the comprehensive data of the 1951 census.

To cover the inter-censal period and to suit the varying needs of different authorities with their diffuse dates of plan preparation and revision, the Registrar General adjusted these projections to allow for net migration to mid-1954 and for planned net migration to mid-1956 in areas containing new towns. The ministry have themselves provided local projections with base dates up to 1959, assuming that the broad mid-1956 age-sex groups would not be significantly affected by the subsequent natural change and migration. Within this context adjustments were made to the 5–14 age groups to take account of the post-war bulge.

This steady flow of the most up-to-date and authoritative information from the ministry to local planning authorities provides a welcome example of co-operation. Unfortunately the projections are not published (why not?), but many will be included in the written analysis accompanying development plans or their reviews, either in their original form or with an allowance for migration. It must be stressed that the projections take into account only the anticipated trends of natural change by births and deaths. The probability of inward and/or outward movements must be assessed by local planning authorities. This appraisal of possible migration is exceedingly complex and involves many planning considerations such as the examination of industrial structure and trends, the availability of housing land, progress with water schemes, the routine of new communications, the improvement of derelict land, etc. From the standpoint of population, the effects of movement are cumulative and exert a greater impact than the straightforward addition or subtraction of potential migrants to or from the population projection. An emigrant population is likely to emphasize the younger age groups of the population, and will take with it the potential births which will have been credited in the projection to the town of departure; its birth rate will be high and its death rate low. The population which remains will tend to have a higher ratio of people in the more elderly age groups, a declining proportion of children to adults, and the acceleration of these symptoms of an ageing population may be at greater than the national rates.[6]

Source material on the migration factor is included in the Census of Population for every district, but not for wards and parishes. The 'balance' figure, which emerges from the differences between natural change through births and deaths and the actual change in total population, may be difficult to interpret as 'migration' in its normal meaning. It refers to comparisons between the enumerated population of two different dates and may therefore not be appropriate in areas with military establishments, where the home-based merchant navy has varied in size, in towns with university students (included at home in 1951 and at college in 1931), or where there has been an increase in the institutional population as by the construction of a new hospital.

For an appreciation of current trends, the electoral roll may be used with some validity for quite small districts. One difficulty is that previous issues may not be available either in the local library or in the electoral office. Changes in numbers will reflect mainly changes in the number of adults, when allowances are made for the number of persons reaching the voting age of 21 (the urban population by yearly age groups of persons from 0 to 21 is included in the 1951 Census of Population) and for the number of deductions from the register by death (Registrar General's *Annual Statistical Review*).

The *Annual Statistical Review* from 1951 onwards may also be used, not as an exact index, but to provide some indication of the annual trends of migration. The method is to compare the mid-year civilian populations of adjacent years; the amount of natural change corrected to place of residence emerges from the difference between the number of births and deaths for the calendar year; the difference between these two sets of data indicates the volume of probable migration. Although the resultant figures should be treated with considerable reserve, the longer the period under examination the greater the validity of the trends which are revealed. The results should anyway be compared with the interpretation of trends from the electoral roll, as a check on the volume and trends of the movement.

These two methods of assessing the volume of migration are derived indirectly from changes in the total population and the figures of births and deaths. The result is expressed in terms of the net balance of movement to or from the area, and is a compound of the total inward and the total outward movements of population. The total size of these two movements does not emerge from either of the previous calculations. Direct statistics on this gross movement into and out of areas were available from national registration and food rationing records from 1948 to 1951, and were supplied to local planning authorities by the ministry. This source ended with the removal of controls and has not been replaced, though it would seem that the exchange of either National Health or National Insurance cards might be used to provide some regular details about the volume, direction and character of the internal movement of population. The 1961 census information on place of former residence should prove most valuable in this respect. A more frequent source of information is however required with some urgency because of the vital place of population movements in planning policy at the national and local levels of administration.

Labour statistics

Two different forms of classification are possible as a person's work may be described either by occupation or by industry. These terms are not synonymous. A van driver can be employed in a cotton mill or by an engineering firm. His occupation, or the nature of the work performed, is the same in each instance; his industry, the end-product of his service or economic activity, is either textiles or metal manufacture. An industrial classification includes persons with a variety of different occupations; the occupational classification cuts across the grouping by industry. This distinction has been incorporated in the census reports since 1911.

The *Standard Industrial Classification* (Central Statistical Office, 1948) contains XXIV main industrial groups, each with its subgroups. It covers all forms of industrial, commercial, professional, service and other economic activity. The unit of classification is the establishment, which includes all premises under the same ownership or management at a particular address, i.e. the workshop, canteen, paint store, accounts office, etc. An exception is made when there are departments engaged in different activities for which separate records of employment, stocks, production, cost, etc. are maintained, an aspect which requires internal information about the organization by the research worker. The establishment is then classified by its principal product or by the type of service rendered; inevitably with the complicated economic activities of British industry there are difficulties, as dual production (an engineering firm producing different types of machinery), subsidiary products (coke from a gas-works) and sub-sections of the firm (as above) cannot be distinguished. Also establishments classified to the same industrial grouping may produce very different products—the building industry includes the small speculative builder and the large national organization—and a particular industrial product may range from the mass-produced item to that individually designed by hand craftsmen. The *Classification of Industries* (General Register Office) shows how each type of industrial undertaking should be classified.

The *Standard Industrial Classification* was revised in 1958 to keep abreast with the changing structure of the economy. Separate headings for cotton, linen and silk were discontinued with the advance of the man-made fibres industry, professional and scientific services including research establishments were separated from their previous industry and made into a new heading, the classification of repair work was altered and the main orders were renumbered and renamed. These alterations will complicate comparisons between the data of the 1951 and 1961 censuses, and interfere with the successive interpretation of inter-censal trends of employment. The history of employment statistics is full of such changes in definition, necessary to improve the quality of the data yet nevertheless creating serious difficulties of interpretation and use.[7]

The *Classification of Occupations* (General Register Office) has likewise been revised 'to take account of new processes and methods in industry which are constantly giving rise to new occupation terms'. The revision took place in 1961, and there will in consequence be difficulties in the comparison of the 1951 and 1961 census data. The new classification has 27 major groups, the basic common factor of all groups being the kind of work done and the nature of the operation performed. Distinctions are also incorporated, as appropriate, when differences result from the material worked in, the degree of skill involved, the physical energy required, the environmental conditions or the social and economic status associated with the occupation.

Four further census classifications are derived from a person's occupation: classification by employment status and classification by economic position, which replace the single classification by industrial status used in the 1951 census, classification by socio-economic group and classification by social class. Employment status distinguishes the 'employee' from the 'self-employed', and further subdivides these two groups. Economic position divides the economically active from the inactive, and there are subdivisions of these two groups. The classification by social class is based on the criterion of the general standing within the community of the occupation concerned and retains the same five major headings as at 1951: the many changes in detail however will invalidate precise comparisons between the 1951 and 1961 censuses; the intermediate, skilled and partly skilled occupations are each further subdivided (at 1961 but not at 1951) into manual, non-manual and agricultural groups to provide eleven divisions in all—a substantial advance in a very useful aid to statistical analysis for distinguishing between the residential characteristics of communities. The remaining classification, that of occupation by socio-economic groups, has also been changed—16 groups at 1961 and 13 at 1951.

These national systems of classification should be used whenever possible in planning surveys as a basis for the grouping of the population. This procedure simplifies communication between members of the profession and the public, and offers greater opportunities for comparative studies. Two examples will clarify the allocation of an occupation to these various classifications. An architect is subgroup 297, 'Surveyors, Architects', of occupational group XXV, 'Professional, Technical Workers, Artists'; he belongs to social class I, 'Professional Occupations', and to socio-economic group 3 or 4, dependent upon whether he is self-employed or working as an employee. A bus driver is grouped in occupational group XIX, 'Transport and Communication Workers', in the manual subdivision of social class III for 'Skilled Occupations', and in socio-economic group 9 for 'Skilled Manual Workers'.

Separate volumes on industry and occupation were published as part of the 1951 Census of Population. The local industrial statistics were based on the area containing the place of work; this is the same method as in 1921, but in 1931, when information collected about the journey to work was not processed, the industrial statistics were based on the area of enumeration; thus the 1931 industrial statistics should never be compared with either the 1921 or the 1951 data. The occupational tables at 1921, 1931 and 1951 were based on the area of enumeration. At 1951, therefore, the census reveals the distribution of occupations primarily by place of residence, whereas the industrial statistics are based on the stated place of work. The tabulations for both industry and occupation show for counties and county boroughs the males and females within each main and subgroup of the two classifications; for lesser districts the industrial and occupational breakdown of both sexes is complete by main headings but is limited to the more important subheadings in each locality.

A further useful census volume is *Usual Residence and Workplace*, known popularly as the 'Journey to Work' report. The classification is compared on the dual basis of place of work and place of residence but, as the smallest unit is the local authority district, the 1951 statistics do not provide a total measure of the gross movement to work. They record only that movement which crosses local authority boundaries. If a suburb lies within a municipality or has been incorporated therein by a boundary extension, then the daily movements to places of employment within the town are not included; if the residential estates exist outside the boundary, the movement is included. The historical accident of the position of the urban boundary influences the coverage of the statistics. Movements within a rural district are not recorded.

The census statistics are concerned primarily with the long-distance journey, though some errors have resulted from the failure of householders to comprehend the questions on the householders' schedule. Lodgings may not have been given as the home address and the head office of the firm or the postal address of the place of work may have been stated instead of the required place of work. Some impossible journeys appear in the tabulations and can be eliminated; other mistakes have been embodied in plausible journeys to influence their accuracy. With these limitations in mind the tabulations show for every district, separately for males and females, the destination of the outward movement of persons resident in the district but working elsewhere, the place of origin of the inward movement of persons working in the district but resident elsewhere and the comparative size of the resident and the day populations.

The practical usefulness of data about the employment characteristics of a locality from the Census of Population is limited by the delays in publication, and by their availability only once in every 10 years. The details are valuable for an appreciation of background trends and conditions; they cannot be used for the study of short-term trends or for the formulation of policy through an appraisal of changing characteristics. For these purposes the research worker must refer to the local employment statistics of the Ministry of Labour. These show the number of persons covered by social insurance schemes, and are divided into the old and the new series. The old series, pre-1948, are not comparable with the new series, because of the major changes in coverage introduced by the National Insurance Act of 1946 and in classification with the compilation of the *Standard Industrial Classification* in 1948. The new series commenced in July 1948 with the introduction of comprehensive insurance for all employed persons aged 15 and over who work for pay or gain. Every such person has an insurance card, to which stamps indicating the weekly contributions are affixed, and these cards are renewed once a year. This renewal, with a quarter of the cards being renewed every three months, permits the analysis and grouping of the insured population. For a variety of technical reasons the quarterly exchange of cards does not represent a random sample of the whole, and the June exchange of cards is supplemented by a compulsory return from all employers of five or more work-people showing the numbers of insurance cards which they hold.

These administrative arrangements influence the quality of the statistics. The information is available for one date in the year, no amendments for seasonal fluctuations are possible in the local data, and only the annual changes between the mid-year estimates are recorded. The figures are of insured employees subdivided into males and females for each industrial order and suborder of the *Standard Industrial Classification*. The coverage is not of the working population because persons who are unemployed, sick, on holiday and on reduced time are included; employers and self-employed, and civil servants who have their contributions paid without the use of cards are excluded from the local figures.

The statistics for Employment Exchange areas are not published, but can be made available through the regional officers of the Ministry of Labour. The local areas to which the figures relate are arbitrary and bear no relationship to district or other boundaries; the area served varies with the closing and opening of exchange offices. The figures denote the number of insured employees classified by the principal product of their establishment; no records are maintained of changes in the classification of establishments, and the classification of any particular establishment is regarded as confidential. Establishments normally make their returns through the nearest employment exchange, but exceptions include the bulk exchange of cards by the central office of organizations with scattered places of work; where possible, and when known, some corrections are made so that the figures relate as closely as possible to the numbers working in each area. A final point is that many insured persons have no fixed place of work—e.g. travellers, building operatives, lorry drivers—and may not report daily to the same address. National statistics of insured employees are published in the Ministry of Labour Gazette.

With the increasing use of these statistics by local planning authorities, the form used now carries the official disclaimer that 'this statement has been prepared solely for the purpose of providing an approximate indication of the industrial structure of the area. The figures are not sufficiently precise to enable comparisons to be made in detail between consecutive years and no significance should be attached to relatively small changes.' Apart from certain supplementary details which may be available through trade unions, employers' federations, bodies such as the Cotton Board, or for particular industries (e.g. agriculture) from their own statistical sources, no other local statistics on this vital planning subject of employment trends are available. There is no alternative but to use these statistics despite their limitations.

Unemployment statistics

The number of persons registered as unemployed at each local office on the second Monday in every month is also available to planning authorities through the Ministry of Labour. The information includes both the wholly unemployed, distinguishing between men, boys, women and girls, and those temporarily out of work, and is usually available on request by age group, duration of unemployment and the industry of last employment. Disabled persons are shown separately. Several difficulties should be noted. The figures cover those who register as unemployed: the inducement to register will vary with the circumstances of the individual, but will be either financial benefit or the possibility of suitable employment. Married women who have opted out of the scheme need not register, and have no incentive to visit an exchange when a dearth of local employment opportunities is known to exist. The level of unemployment usually declines during holiday and wakes weeks; persons not in work but receiving a guaranteed minimum wage, such as dock workers under the National Dock Labour Scheme, do not register; a trawlerman may register as unemployed in the short shore period between fishing trips. The register cannot be regarded as listing those in 'involuntary idleness'.

The measure of a derived rate of unemployment is suspect because the numerator, the total number of registered unemployed, and the denominator, the total number of insured employees, are not comparable. The number of insured persons relates to the preceding June, whereas unemployment is estimated month by month with no time lag. Further, employment data are based on the exchange of books at the office nearest to place of work in contrast with the freedom to register as unemployed anywhere—typically by place of residence, though a move to a locality with better prospects of work may be undertaken. The ratio is thus statistically unreliable. Turner, after measuring the accuracy of the index of unemployment for the Lancashire textile recession of 1952, exposed its deficiencies. 'First, it recorded only part of those affected by partial employment . . . Second, it did not fully record the number of people quite deprived of employment. Third, it became especially incomplete in what may well have been the critical months . . . And finally, the registration did not fluctuate solely in inverse relation to the level of employment.'[8]

The number of 'employment vacancies' for men, women and juveniles is also available monthly for each employment exchange area; the details provide a useful comparison in a continuous series with the statistics of unemployment. A vacancy includes labour requirements reported to the exchanges by employers; as the labour force may be obtained by other means, or as the firm may not change its labour demands lodged with the Ministry of Labour if trading conditions alter, the index does not pretend to be exact. It remains useful however as a guide to changes in the labour situation. The factory inspectorate, a department of the Ministry of Labour, have details of each factory, giving its address, the numbers employed and its trading activity; the data are confidential to local planning authorities.

Housing statistics

The Census of Population provides information about housing at the district level, and gives the total of the population in private households and the number of structurally separate dwellings occupied for wards and parishes. The source is the information provided by the householders' schedules; there has been no national survey of housing as such post-war. By contrast the American Census of Housing in 1940 and 1950 enumerated some 28 items on dwellings and their households. These included conversions, structural type, exterior materials, year built, value of the property, mortgage status, condition of repair and colour or race of head of household. These data were obtained for every urban and rural dwelling, and tabulated for each community. No such comprehensive coverage is available for England and Wales, where district details are classified in the county volumes of the 1951 census according to the number of rooms, their density of occupation by the number of people and families occupying houses of different sizes, and the availability of certain household arrangements; the subject of rented accommodation was included in addition at 1961.

The understanding of the tabulations involves knowledge of the definitions. At 1951 the enumerated population was divided into non-private households and private households. The former included 'all persons enumerated in hotels, boarding houses and institutions or otherwise grouped in establishments for some functional purpose', including educational establishments, homes of various types, hospitals, defence establishments, places of detention and miscellaneous community establishments. Boarding and lodging houses have always proved difficult to classify; the method adopted at 1951 was that 'boarding houses are non-private households when so described, or when the number of boarders exceeds the number of the householder's family', a definition which must lead to certain anomalies.

Private households form the remainder of the population. As already suggested a comparison of the total population in private households is possible for parishes and wards, and this may be more appropriate than comparisons between enumerated populations as an indication of local population trends. A private household is defined as 'single persons living alone or groups of individuals voluntarily living together under a single menage in the sense of sharing the same living-room or eating at the same table; boarders and domestic servants are included in the household with which they were enumerated, as also are visitors'. This concept of a census household is not the same as the family unit. Two separate families sharing one house count as one household for census purposes, and the word voluntarily may be a misnomer—this fact has not been established by the census schedule and the word should be omitted from the definition.

The concept of a structurally separate dwelling is 'any room or suite of rooms intended or used for habitation having separate access to the street, or to a common landing or staircase'. This represents the ordinary meaning which attaches to a house, flat or maisonette; it includes as a dwelling a houseboat or caravan if occupied on census night, but not otherwise. It excludes the large house which has not been structurally subdivided but which is shared by more than one family. The number of vacant dwellings, distinguishing between furnished and others, was also recorded at 1951; the details were recorded by the census enumerator but no definition is included in the county volumes.

A room is defined as the usual living-rooms including bedrooms, but excluding sculleries, landings, lobbies, closets, office- and shop-rooms. As the intention is to include rooms in which the household live, eat or sleep, the kitchen is included if meals are eaten there but not otherwise—an arbitrary distinction which must lead to differences in classification between identical houses. With regard to the measure of rooms in a dwelling, the greater use of through-rooms and houses with lounge-halls make a consistent and uniform classification difficult; also, variations in the size of rooms does not influence the classification. Possession or otherwise of a garage, or garage space, and the size of gardens is not recorded.

The quality of the building, e.g. by age or by rateable value, is not covered in the census though some indication of habitability is provided by the possession of household arrangements. The distinction is made between all households and households sharing dwellings having exclusive use, households sharing with another household and households entirely without the five normally accepted amenities of a kitchen sink, piped water, cooking stove, water closet and fixed bath. Each item is shown separately, and certain of the arrangements (e.g. the exclusive use of stove and sink) are noted in conjunction with each other. For urban areas with a population of over 50,000 persons, further distinctions are made by household size and by the number of occupied rooms.

'Apart from the Population Censuses there are no complete records of the number of houses. The question of estimating the total number in existence for other than census years is of consider-able importance. At first sight making such estimates would seem to be easy . . . The number of houses must be equal to the total counted at the preceding census plus new houses built since then, plus the net addition . . . due to conversion, minus the number of dwellings demolished and minus the transfer of houses to non-residential purposes . . . If only we could find the numbers, the arithmetic would be easy.'[9] This desirable range of detail is not available at either the local or the national levels.

The principal inter-censal source of information is the *Housing Return*, published quarterly by the Ministry of Housing and Local Government from information supplied by local authorities to show houses completed and houses demolished by 'local authority areas'. Each of these three terms has its difficulties of interpretation. The number of new houses is given as a cumulative figure since April 1945 and covers only new permanent houses; temporary houses and residential caravans are excluded, as are additions to the stock of housing by conversions. The concept of 'local authority area' has a dual meaning according to the type of house; local authority houses are shown against the area of the local authority building the houses whether they are erected inside or outside that area; houses built by private builders are shown against the authority in whose area they are situated; the number of new permanent houses constructed in each local authority area cannot therefore be determined from this source. Demolitions, as a cumulative total from January 1955, distinguish between demolitions under the Housing Act of 1957 and the demolition of other unfit houses; dwellings removed to make way for other development such as commercial or university expansion, road improvement schemes, or by conversions to uses such as offices are not recorded.

The rating registers contain statistics about the houses in local authority areas, classified by rateable value and distinguishing between owner-occupier, rented privately and local authority dwellings. This fund of local information has to be collected from each authority separately as there is no central compilation of these facts. The rateable values of houses may provide a comparative indication of their quality, though the index is not infallible as large houses with a high net annual value may be of poor quality and vice versa. As houses becoming vacant and occupied are notified to the rating authority it should be possible to use this source to indicate additions to the number of houses, the wastage and the number of vacant premises. A regular return of this information to the Ministry of Housing and Local Government, and the inclusion of all the details in an enlarged annual rather than quarterly *Housing Return*, should overcome the deficiencies in housing statistics to which reference has been made. Housing is recognized as an urgent problem to which the planning profession have many responsibilities; statistics to provide a complete and up-to-date coverage of the position should be more readily available to assist in the elucidation of the facts.

The *Housing Return* has been seen to indicate the progress of slum clearance. It is important to note that the total of local authority slum clearance proposals, often quoted as a measure of the size of the problem, provides nothing more than a guide to the intentions of local authorities in their clearance programmes. The figures are not necessarily based on any survey and should not be used to measure the total number of houses which are unfit for habitation. Housing provides an excellent example of a subject where the faulty interpretation of the statistics, through the failure to appreciate their coverage and limitations, clouds the magnitude of the great planning problem of urban renewal which must still be tackled in many cities.

A further factor in the housing situation is the demand for housing accommodation through changes in population size and composition. 'This number depends entirely on the number of households and these, in turn, express their demand through the heads of households who normally own or rent a house. These heads may be heads of families, members of a group of people living together, or persons living alone.'[10] The number may be estimated for each district on certain assumptions from the census data about households. The actual number of households can then be projected forward to indicate the number of potential households on the hypothesis, suggested from a comparison of the housing statistics at the 1931 and 1951 censuses, that the proportion of heads of private households in the main population groups will be constant. These very important projections, so vital to long-term planning, have been prepared by the Ministry of Housing and Local Government and were supplied to local planning authorities in 1960 to show the estimated number of households at mid-1959 and mid-1971. The method must rely on various assumptions and is admitted to be 'rather crude', but refinements can be introduced as sample surveys and the 1961 census of population provide additional facts. In the meantime the statistics will prove invaluable for the quinquennial reviews of the development plans. They provide an inspiring illustration of the provision of fundamental information by the ministry to the local planning authorities responsible for the preparation of policy statements in their development plans. It will be interesting to see whether the land zoned for housing will equal anticipated demand from changes in age-sex structure of the population.

Other statistical sources

Many other statistical sources may require to be interpreted by planning authorities. The following list does not purport to be exhaustive.

There have been various *Censuses of Production* since 1907. The present position is a census every three years and intermediate annual samples by the Board of Trade. The statistics disclose the number of establishments in each industry, their output, the use of materials and fuels, wages and salaries, stocks and capital expenditure. They provide essential planning facts for the economic analysis of a particular industry at the national level, and can be used to calculate various indices to distinguish between the concept of heavy and light industry.[11] Because of the confidentiality of the returns, no local statistics can be published or disclosed.

The first *Census of Distribution* was undertaken by the Board of Trade in 1951, and covered trade during 1950 in the principal retail and closely associated service trades. The local details are published in vol. I, 'Retail and Service Trades: Area Tables'. Information for towns with a population of 2,500 or over covers in total only the number of establishments, sales, full-time male and female staff, part-time employees, and wages and salaries. For towns with a population of 25,000 and over, the above information is provided for each of the various categories of the retail and service trades, e.g. grocery, clothing, hardware, furniture, chemists. The coverage of the survey was incomplete as many small traders did not make returns, and the coverage of sales is of all business undertaken in each establishment irrespective of its classification. The details have been found to be most valuable in connection with the classification of towns, their spheres of influence, and by New Town Development Corporations to assess their central area shopping provision. A second census, relating to trade in 1961, will be undertaken during 1962. The approach will be to all small retailers with a turnover of £5,000 or less; all other independent retailers employing less than 25 persons will answer the same range of questions as the small retailers, whilst a 10 per cent sample of this group will respond to further questions; large retail organizations will be asked more questions again.[12]

The *Conurbation volume* of the Census of Population provides overall statistics for these urban agglomerations, which would otherwise have to be grouped together for the relevant local authority areas. The data are comparable with those of the county volumes and include population, area, dwellings, rooms, households, birthplace, age, education and social class, but not industry, occupation and journey to work. The definitions are as previously discussed, and the value of these statistics hence depends on the statistical concept of a conurbation. The fundamental definition, as statistics are tabulated only for the administrative areas of local authorities, is that conurbations should be an aggregate of local authority units. Further relevant considerations were that these areas should be continually built up, that local areas strongly attached to a centre for work, shopping, higher education, sports or entertainment should be included, and some consideration should be given to population density. Finally, where two or more areas could be defined on the basis of the above definitions, then the larger area should be selected. The delimited census areas are for the purposes of statistical comparison only, and are not necessarily the 'conurbation areas' which might be suitable for administrative reform or as regional planning units. The tendency to make use of the census localities for these other purposes is to be deplored. For instance, when a rural district lies adjacent to a continuously built-up area, the developed area is excluded from the boundary of the 'census' conurbation if the greater part of the area enjoys a lower population density; it may for other purposes be regarded as an integral part of the conurbation.

The *Ministry of Labour Gazette,* the monthly journal of the Ministry of Labour, contains national information on average earnings and hours for groups of industries, and wage rates; industrial disputes with causes, durations and results; labour turnover, i.e. the numbers taken on and discharged from certain industries each month; and the number of vacancies known to employment exchanges. Further statistics, such as the figures of hours worked in industry, appear at less frequent intervals. A

Guide to Statistics collected by H. M. Factory Inspectorate was published by the Ministry of Labour through H.M.S.O. in 1960.

Labour statistics of a different type, unpublished regional statistics on the *building labour force*, were made available to local planning authorities through the Ministry of Housing and Local Government for the preparation of the 1951 Development Plans. Collected initially by the Ministry of Works and based on contractors' returns, the statistics provided a break-down of the total building labour force between different development activities such as new housing, housing repairs, educational buildings, industry, etc., and the output of each activity was expressed in terms of £'s per man-month. These productivity statistics were regarded as vital to the formulation of a realistic development plan, and were particularly necessary for the phasing of development, for the costing of proposals, and for assessing the financial implications of the proposed development. These data are no longer available as site returns are not now made, but the importance of these statistics to objective planning would justify a quinquennial series of sample surveys in each region to provide the requisite information.

The *Board of Trade* provide information to local planning authorities about applications which have been approved for an Industrial Development Certificate. The requirements were changed by the Local Employment Act 1960 to restrict comparisons; subsequently, these returns give the I.D.C. approvals within each local authority area distinguishing between new development, extensions, repeat I.D.C.s, and changes of use. The floor area in square feet, the estimated additional male and female employment to be provided, the date of the certificate and the industrial classification of the approved development is shown. These details are confidential to local planning authorities for their official use and should not be disclosed.

The most comprehensive source on *road statistics* is the annual publication of the British Road Federation, *Basic Road Statistics*, which brings together much of the published national details on road traffic and transport to provide an excellent example of a reliable statistical source by a non-government body. The statistics are continuous and cover *inter alia* the number of licensed vehicles with annual figures from 1904, the number of new registrations, certain comparative information about people per car and traffic densities elsewhere, road casualties from 1928 and the cost to the community of road accidents, employees in road transport and, as befits their crusade for better roads, details of road expenditure in contrast with the receipts from motor taxation.

For local information the Ministry of Transport publish annually *Mechanically Propelled Motor Vehicles*. This provides details of the number of vehicles for which licences were current during the quarter ending 30 September, the peak season for the registration of vehicles. The break-down of information is into the different types of vehicle and is by licensing authority area, i.e. by the place where the vehicle is normally kept or garaged (not place of work) in county boroughs and administrative counties.

National traffic surveys undertaken by the Ministry of Transport have not been published post-war, though the information is usually available on request. The latest comprehensive information on traffic flow is the National Traffic Census of 1954; subsequent checks include the continuous 50-point census by the Road Research Laboratory and the annual August censuses of the Ministry of Transport at 100 points. These data are used to provide traffic indices to show the rate of vehicle growth. Official censuses are based usually on the flow of vehicles past a census point for the 16 hours from 6 a.m. to 10 p.m. on each of seven consecutive days. The local details of accidents are available in police records, and are best plotted on base maps to indicate 'black spots' for improvement.

An annual agricultural census is taken on 4 June; the results are published in *Agricultural Statistics*. The return is compulsory from 'occupiers of an agricultural holding of more than one acre in extent'. The purpose of the return is to assess the crop and livestock production of the country, and it must be used with caution as a record of the changing pattern of rural land use. For example, the returns do not cover the total area of each holding but the fields actually used for growing agricultural and horticultural products, or under fallow; woodlands and private gardens would be excluded and grazing land rented from a golf course would be included. The area covered by the farmhouse, farm buildings, roads and small quarries is not shown. The published data are for counties and shows the acreage of agricultural land, the area under the principal crops, the number and description of livestock and the number of persons employed; provided confidentiality is not involved, these statistics are summarized by parishes and this data, though not published, can generally be made available to research workers. The Forestry Commission undertook a survey of woodlands between 1947 and 1949, covering all woodlands of over five acres in extent; a 1 per cent sample of woods of one to five acres in extent was surveyed in 1951.[13]

Certain national statistics of planning importance are tabulated in the appendices to the *Annual Reports of the Ministry of Housing and Local Government*. These include some summary information, *inter alia*, about local government finance, valuation, grants and loans, development plan submissions and approvals, appeal decisions and progress with the New Towns. Certain local authorities, e.g. Birmingham and Lancashire, publish regular statistical series.

Conclusion

Neat tabulations of statistics present the appearance of impeccable accuracy. The integrity of the compilers is not in doubt but 'it is rare indeed to find a piece of statistical information that is "perfect", in the double sense of being observed without error and of being precisely suited to its purpose. Even the elaborate and expensive organization of a census of population can never tell you exactly how many people were in the country on the census night; still less can it tell you what you usually want to know, the population "normally resident" in an area . . . The qualifications which the honest originator had in mind, and perhaps stated in small type at the foot of his tables, have been forgotten. "This," the final user seems to say, "is the only estimate I can find. Better the moonlight than complete darkness: let us hope that the errors will cancel out." '[14]

It is sound advice to be suspicious, rather than to accept statistics at their face value. Facts must be understood before they can be handled intelligently and, if the method of collection and the significance of definitions are not appreciated, then conclusions which emerge from a study of the statistical sources must themselves be suspect. Some understanding of statistical limitations must form part of the training of a planner for this very reason. He must either be able to interpret the data competently himself, or be aware of this deficiency and be willing to rely on appropriate advice. No intermediate course is possible.

1   R. L. Collison, *Library Assistance to Readers*, 1960.

2   Town Planning Institute, *Planning Research*, 1961.

3   E. Devons, *An Introduction to British Economic Statistics*, 1956; C. F. Carter and A. D. Roy, *British Economic Statistics*, 1954; M. G. Kendall (ed.), *The Sources and Nature of the Statistics of the United Kingdom*, vol. I, 1952, and vol. II, 1957; H. M. Treasury, *Government Statistical Services*, H.M.S.O., 1953; Inter-Departmental Committee on Social and Economic Research, *Guides to Official Sources*, H.M.S.O.: 1. Labour Statistics, 2. Census Reports of Great Britain, 1801–1931, 3. Local Government Statistics, 4. Agriculture and Food Statistics, 5. Social Security Statistics; *Studies in Official Statistics*, H.M.S.O.: 4. The Length of Working Life of Males in Great Britain, 5. New Contributions to Economic Statistics.

4   Sections 9(1) and 9(5) respectively.

5   Ministry of Housing and Local Government, *Population*, Technical Memorandum No. 4, 1955 (unpublished), and *Guide to the Use of Local Population Statistics* (supplement to the above), 1956. J. R. L. Schneider, 'Local Population Projections in England and Wales', *Population Studies*, vol. X, no. 1, 1956. P. Cox, 'Estimating the Future Population', *Applied Statistics*, vol. I, 1952, pp. 82–94.

6   M. P. Newton and J. R. Jeffery, *Internal Migration: Some Aspects of Population Movements within England and Wales*, H.M.S.O., 1951.

7   J. Bellamy reclassifies all occupational information since 1841 in 'Occupations in Kingston upon Hull', *Yorkshire Bulletin of Economic and Social Research*, vol. IV, no. 1, 1952, pp. 46–50.

8   H. A. Turner, 'Measuring Unemployment', *Journal of the Royal Statistical Society*, series A, vol. 118, 1955, p. 45. See also D. Bailey, 'Note on British Unemployment Statistics', *Applied Statistics*, vol. IX, 1960, pp. 51–9.
    M. Bowley in M. G. Kendall, op. cit., vol. I, p. 306.

10 Ministry of Housing and Local Government, *Estimating the Number of Houses Required*, 1960 (unpublished).

11 F. S. Florence, *Investment, Location and Size of Plant*, 1948. A *Guide to Official Sources* no. 6 on the Census of Production is in the course of preparation.

12 *Board of Trade Journal*, 29 August 1953, pp. 425–8; D. A. Clark, 'The Census of Distribution', *Applied Statistics*, vol. II, no. 1, 1953, pp. 1–12; '1961 Census', *Board of Trade Journal*, 29 September 1960.

13 Forestry Commission, *Census Report no. 1: Census of Woodlands 1947–1949: Woodlands of Five Acres and Over*, H.M.S.O., 1952; *Census Report no. 2: Hedgerow and Park Timber and Woods under Five Acres 1951*, H.M.S.O., 1953.

14 Carter and Roy, op. cit., p.113.

American bibliographies

The *Exchange Bibliographies* of the Committee (now Council) of Planning Librarians, 6318 Thornhill Drive, Oakland 11, California, contain references to international planning material. A recent comprehensive bibliography is G. C. Bestor and H. R. Jones, *City Planning: A Basic Bibliography of Sources and Trends*, California Council of Civil Engineers and Land Surveyors, 1962. Some bibliographies on specialist subjects include B. J. L. Berry, and A. Pred, *Central Place Studies: a Bibliography of Theory and Applications*, Regional Science Research Institute, 1961; Bureau of Public Roads, *Bibliography on Metropolitan Areas*, 1958; G. M. McMannon, *A Survey of the Literature on Industrial Location*, Business Research Centre, Syracuse University, 1959; W. A. Pillsbury, *The Economic and Social Effects of Highway Improvement: an annotated bibliography*, Virginia Council of Highway Investigation, 1961; U.S. Dept. of Agriculture, *Urbanization and Changing Land Uses: a bibliography of selected References 1950–1958*, 1960.

3
SAMPLING, INTERVIEWS AND QUESTIONNAIRES

FEW planning investigations can be completed from the study of existing tabulations alone. The range of available facts may have proved of value in the elucidation of trends or in the provision of salient background detail, and regional or local characteristics may have been discerned in contrast with the national tendency. In most instances field surveys will have to be undertaken to yield precise evidence on particular aspects of the problem under investigation and, in this more intimate approach, interviews, questionnaires and direct observation each have much to contribute. Few subjects can be studied by one method alone; most require a combination of field techniques for their understanding. The first stage is invariably the selection of the population to be surveyed, population being used in its statistical sense of survey units such as factories, motor vehicles, people, etc.

Random sampling

Knowledge of random sampling is part of the *vade-mecum* of all research workers; without its benefits he becomes lost in a mass of data which does not contribute more to the understanding of a problem than the objective analysis of a smaller volume of material collected by random means. Seebohm Rowntree, in his early study of poverty in York, covered every wage-earning family.[1] Advances in methodology have out-dated this 'census-type' approach, which is usually a practical impossibility on the grounds of time and cost alone. The more usual present technique is to select a proportion of the total population from which the characteristics of the whole can be inferred. The population to be surveyed must be representative of the whole; it must be chosen on the methodical basis of a rigorous statistical approach. This precise method involves the careful use of sampling techniques. The population is selected at random, and not arbitrarily or by some haphazard means which may involve personal prejudice or preconceived ideas.

Sampling does not reduce, but can enhance, the accuracy of a survey. This apparent antithesis results from the fact that the handling of smaller numbers permits the collection of more detailed information and more supervision at each stage of the inquiry. Much more can be learned from one interview of 30 minutes than from six superficial meetings each of five minutes. Smaller numbers have to be handled throughout the survey at all stages from collection throughout processing to analysis. The cost of the investigation in terms of time, cost, labour and inconvenience to the population being surveyed are all reduced. These represent considerable advantages in exchange for the rigid application to the survey of the laws of probability. The method of approach is a skilled procedure which must be designed carefully and followed through systematically. The use of sampling in the 1961 Census of Population, when only one-tenth of householders were asked to complete the full range of questions, should assist in 'popularizing' the use of sampling. In America sampling is used to check on the accuracy of this Census of Population. (See note on p. 84.)

A sample must avoid bias in the selection of the population. The choice must not be influenced by human preference, but must be predetermined in such a way that each unit enjoys an equal or known chance of selection. No section or group can be favoured, the sample should be representative. This equal chance of selection can be achieved by one of three basic methods. The first, the principle of the church raffle, is where each member of the population has a number, these are well mixed, and a predetermined number of numbers are withdrawn. Alternatively the sample units can be selected from tables of random sample numbers which, in essence, are numbers selected by random means from a previously conducted draw.[2] Thirdly, a random starting point is selected from a list and then every 'n'th member of the population is interviewed, e.g. numbers 3, 13, 23, etc., on a rating, voting or housing list. The subject of possible lists or sampling frames will be returned to subsequently.

Precision can be increased by the introduction of stratification *before* the selection of a random sample within each group. Thus the records of a housing authority can be divided by the type of house or the rating register by premises of different rateable value *before* the random sample is chosen from within each of these pre-selected groups. This method, stratified random sampling, ensures that each distinct group is represented in the coverage of the sample and the varying characteristics within these groups may then be examined. The random sample can be in the same proportion in each stratum, or can vary relatively from stratum to stratum. A variable sampling fraction is usual when numbers in each stratum differ, or when a wide range of composition exists within any one stratum; smaller numbers or a greater variation would normally necessitate a proportionately larger sample. The results from within each stratum must, of course, be weighted to arrive at the overall estimate of population characteristics.

Stratification provides a gain in precision, but also becomes necessary because the results for each stratum may be more significant than for the total population. One may be interested not in the attitudes of families living on a local authority estate, but in the relative attitudes of tenants in flats, maisonettes, semi-detached and terrace houses. Each stratum may be further divided before the sample is selected, for example, as in the above illustration, into units of two, three and four bedrooms; indeed further subdivisions of the stratum might be appropriate such as the physical situation adjacent to a main estate road, around a green, or on a cul-de-sac. Subcategories of the smaller-sized groups do however present fewer possibilities of detailed analysis. The essential sampling requirement is that information for stratification and for further subdivision must be available before the collection of data can commence and, therefore, the necessary details must be recognizable from the sampling frame, list or group from which the sample is selected. It would therefore be impossible to stratify families on the above housing estate by total family income or by occupation or by religion, unless it so happens that these details are disclosed on the authority's housing application form.

How then does one select the appropriate stratification? It is only possible to stratify by a factor when this characteristic can be identified in *every* unit of the sample population; this prerequisite does, in practice, severely limit the amount of stratification which is feasible. The stratification factor must have some relevance to the topic under investigation, otherwise no benefit in precision is bestowed. Where the size of the sample does not warrant multiple stratification then the single stratification thought to be the most significant should be adopted, a choice which in its turn demands knowledge of the subject-matter and which may itself require pilot surveys to reveal the most significant groups in the population.

The ability or otherwise to stratify before the selection of the random sample does not prevent the grouping of data *after* the collection of survey information. Thus the income of families, if unknown before the survey, may vitally affect family attitudes or characteristics. The evidence from the survey may be reclassified against various income groups to determine the significance of this factor. This regrouping of data against a large number of different possible factors provides a most important method of planning analysis; it furnishes an example of that continual search for relationships between different groups of data which is the hall-mark of the good research worker. Fact finding and collecting exist as but one small facet of the research process.

Sampling frames

Random sampling involves selection from some form of sample frame, and those most frequently used are lists, registers and maps either in isolation or in conjunction with each other. The essential requirements are that the frame must cover the whole population, must be complete (i.e. exclude no one), avoid duplication (i.e. include no one twice), be accurate and up-to-date, and be accessible and available for use by the sampler. Any omission in any of these categories must be rectified before sampling can begin. Income tax returns, census schedules and employers' returns to the Ministry of Labour cannot be used because of their confidentiality; the most used sources have restrictions on their use which present their own specific difficulties and problems of method.

Maps can be used for area sampling, but must be up-to-date. Cartographic revision is normally desirable before large-scale plans can be used. If stratification is required the city area can be divided up into blocks of buildings, such as the small areas used for the calculation of net densities and shown on the six inch to the mile town map submissions of local planning authorities. The blocks are numbered and a random sample can be selected. Within each selected block, the residential buildings are listed, and a random sample made of the requisite number of houses to be visited. In a city perhaps one block in 50 could be selected, and then say one house in 10 in each block.

In a smaller area such as a residential estate a valid method would be to devise an itinerary which visits every dwelling in the locality. Every 'n'th house could then be selected for interview. Either of these two methods involving maps as a sample frame would satisfy fully the basic requirement that each house in the survey area should have an equal chance of selection; no element of personal bias or preference has intruded into the selection. The canons of the scientific approach have been maintained.

An interesting example of the above techniques in the use of maps for sampling is provided by a 'systematic area sample' of the British road system.[3] The requirements were for about 1,000 census points, with some additional weight being given to the more important roads. The sample was selected by providing a physical coverage of the country on 1:25,000 scale ordnance survey sheets. The initial sample was selected by the systematic placing of short lines on a grid overlay, superimposing these predetermined lines over each ordnance sheet, and listing all the points where one of these lines cut across a road. These data were then stratified into eighty strata on the basis of ten regions and eight classes of road, and the selection of the final sample was at every 'n'th point from this list. Maps are also frequently used in agricultural and crop surveys, and provided the sampling frame for the 1942 Census of

Woodlands in England and Wales. Similar methods could be adopted for local studies of traffic movement and generation.

The *electoral register* is frequently used as a sample frame in social surveys, an illustration being provided from a recent study in Bethnal Green.[4] A random sample of the adult population was drawn from the electoral register by selecting every 36th name from the 40,487 names on this voting list. This coverage of 2·8 per cent was chosen to yield about 1,000 interviews, a number fixed by financial considerations. As the survey was of private households, persons living in hospitals as private families were excluded. For more detailed interviewing a subsample was drawn from the 152 parents of two or more children in the general sample; the selection of the required 1:3 persons was then achieved by giving each individual a serial number, these numbers were placed in a container and 50 were drawn out at random. All the facts presented in the body of the survey report depend for their general validity on these techniques of initial selection. An important point of principle is that survey reports should include a discussion of the method of approach. Bias in this preparatory work will invalidate the findings of the field survey; reviewers should comment first on method, and then on conclusions.

The Register of Electors is prepared annually against a qualifying date in October and is in force from February of the subsequent year.[5] It is not revised, and thus its age ranges from four months when published to 16 months at the end of its life; there are losses to the register by death and by removal, and gains by immigration. It records civilian local government voters, and distinguishes separately ('L') property owners resident outside the area (i.e. having a local government vote, but not a parliamentary vote, through this factor), service voters ('S'), and electors coming of age before 1 June in the year after the qualifying date ('Y'), i.e. the register shows persons aged over 20 years 5 months at the qualifying date. The register is prepared for polling districts in the parliamentary boroughs, and is broken down into wards and parishes. Within each urban polling district it lists streets alphabetically, in each street houses are arranged numerically in sequence along each side of the street, and at each address the electors are listed alphabetically (i.e. the head of the family is not necessarily first) in the order of their surnames and, within surname, by forename. Persons registered are those qualified to vote; they must therefore be British subjects, resident in the area and have reached the age of 21 on the qualifying date. The exclusions may affect the validity of the register for sampling purposes in certain areas, e.g. aliens in certain inner urban districts and young households where both parents are 'under age' in some new residential districts.

The register may be stratified either by locality, i.e. by taking a random selection of polling districts, or streets. If sampling is to be of individuals every 'n'th name can be selected after eliminating (or consciously including) service voters and property owners; males and females can usually be distinguished by their first names. If one requires to interview a particular group within a town, e.g. old persons of families with children, then select the sample as previously, contact these persons, interview only those who fall within the required category, and discard the others. There is no alternative to this tedious and wasteful approach, unless a complete list of the required group exists. If an interview sample of 1,000 persons is required and if one in four of the adult population are thought to fall within the required group, then 4,000 persons should be selected in the initial sample from the register.

The sample may also be of addresses. The correct method is to select every 'n'th elector, and to note the address together with the total number of voters at this address. The more voters the greater the probability of selection and, therefore, to eliminate this emphasis, the final sample should include every address containing one name, half the addresses containing two names, a third of the addresses containing three names, and so on.

Rating records can be used in a similar manner to the register of electors. These are not held centrally at libraries, and must be consulted by arrangement in the rating office of district councils (county and municipal boroughs, urban and rural districts; N.B. county councils are not rating authorities). The records are usually in alphabetical street order within wards, and show the type of property (house, flat, shop), its rateable value, and the name of the owner and of the occupier. They should provide a complete and up-to-date list of dwellings, with stratification being possible by locality, rateable value, or by tenant and owner-occupier. The random sample could select every 'n'th address, but these need to be converted into households as any address may contain one or more household. The usual method is, if the sample address contains two households then both are interviewed and the next household on the list is omitted; if three households, again all are interviewed and the next two addresses on the list are rejected, and so on. Precise definitions of the term 'household' must precede this selection for interview.

Because the rating records can only be consulted locally, their greatest use is for sampling within towns. Sampling in a region or a conurbation would prove a laborious exercise by this frame. On the other hand the rating records are more accurate than the electoral register, because a house is rated as soon as it is occupied and revision is continuous. It is thus more useful, especially in areas of change or of new developments. If arrangements can be made for the rating officer to record alterations in the occupation of premises, then the character of the inward and outward movements, which may be of vital importance for planning purposes, can be studied by sampling techniques. More valuable stratifications by quality and by type are also feasible with no difficulty.

Maps, the electoral register and rating records do not complete the number of possible sampling frames. Any list, provided it fulfils the stated requirements, may be used. Examples include the housing records of local authorities which are usually arranged by streets, the wage cards of employees, members of a trade association, classified directories, or lists of hotel and boarding accommodation. The temptation to select a sample from a group which is conveniently brought together must be avoided or, if studied, its limitations must be appreciated. Manufacturers belonging to a trade organization need not be representative of all manufacturing interests, just as old people living in homes are not typical of all old people.

An example of the use of a special list is provided by a Ministry of Transport survey into the amount and nature of the work performed by licensed goods vehicles.[6] The sampling frame in this instance was the 'Goods Vehicles Index', a list kept in the area offices of the licensing authorities for goods vehicles. Stratification was by region and by types of vehicle and, after selection, a form was sent to the owner of each vehicle for completion.

Nor need the sample frame always be a list in the form so far discussed. It could be the flow of vehicles along a road stratified by the type of vehicle, or the movement of customers from a shop, or vehicles parked in a locality. Whatever the problem some form of random sampling method can be devised to reduce the volume of survey work to a manageable proportion which can be handled with available resources. 'The methods employed must be thoroughly sound, theoretically and practically, both in order that satisfactory results may be ensured, and also in order that mistrust cannot subsequently be engendered by criticism of the methods adopted. It must never be forgotten that it is not sufficient to provide results which are in fact correct. They must also be generally accepted if they are to have their full value.'[7]

Sample size and non-response

A point not so far mentioned is the size of the sample. Numbers by themselves or the proportion of the population included in the sample are not important; a sample does not gain in accuracy when the numbers are increased if the selection procedure is in anyway biased or faulty. Quantity can never replace quality, size does not eliminate errors, and mere numbers to impress provide nothing more than a spurious sense of authenticity. Statistically the required size of the sample depends upon the limits of error which can be tolerated, and this factor must be calculated separately for each stratum in stratified sampling. In practice the most desirable size is restricted by reasons of cost, time or manpower. A compromise is often necessary between the ideal and the practicable. The responsibility of the sampler is to obtain the best results within the limitations of the available resources.

Surveys are democratic; the subject has the right to refuse co-operation. At Bethnal Green there were 10 per cent of non-contacts in the sample drawn, and 5·5 per cent of refusals in the number interviewed; in the national survey of goods vehicles 2 per cent of the forms were not returned.[8] It cannot be assumed that the missing elements will have the same characteristics as those who respond. Non-response may be motivated by some special attribute which requires to be understood if the survey is to be complete. It is not something to be dismissed as of no consequence. Working house-wives and male wage-earners on night work may, for example, prove difficult to interview.

The method of dealing with the problem depends on the type of non-response. If the unit has ceased to exist, e.g. a house is no longer occupied or a tenant has died, it may be eliminated from the survey and replaced by a randomly selected substitute. Where people have moved, the new group may be substituted. Every effort by perseverance, tact and through a series of repeated calls at different times on various days should be made to reduce the remaining non-response to the minimum hard core of refusals. For this recalcitrant group, although the answers to some questions must remain in the 'unknown' category, a substantial amount of factual detail (age, sex, occupation, place of work, method of travel) can be obtained from neighbours, rent-collectors or by observation. The experience of most investigators is that the vast majority of people are only too willing to be interviewed and to describe their feelings and reactions, especially when the subject as in planning can be shown to have a practical importance—reactions to a new house, relationship between home and workplace, or the demand for community facilities. A belief in the reasons for the survey by the interviewer is one of the most effective answers to the non-response of certain individuals.

Much more use should be made of sampling methods in planning research. A vast range of problems lack the factual information necessary for their understanding and intelligent solution. Best, for example, has referred to the need for improving our land-use records. 'In order to obtain a statement of the total extent of land in different uses at different times, it is not always really necessary to measure and record every single piece of land in that particular category. By using sampling methods, an estimate of the area can often be calculated. For example, the urban land use of smaller settlements has not usually been surveyed by planning departments

—a stratified sample of such settlements could be selected and their land use (or other characteristics) studied in some detail. The sample information can then be adjusted to obtain estimates of land use for the country as a whole.'[9]

The preceding text provides nothing more than an introduction to certain of the salient characteristics of random or probability sampling. The purpose has been to inspire a greater use and confidence in this method of scientific investigation and its application to planning problems. No reference has been made to mathematical formulae, to sampling distributions, to the standard error of the mean, or to the estimation of limits of confidence. The emphasis has been on the method of approach which, if intelligently applied, can be used with considerable advantage in many different survey situations to yield an unbiased and representative group for study.

The validity of sampling may be checked when a complete survey has been undertaken. Thus Rowntree, in the report of his second survey of York, selected systematically every tenth interview schedule and compared the results with those obtained for all cases.[10] The same method was used for samples of 1 in 20, 30, 40 and 50 to show that comparable results were attained, irrespective of the size of the sample. Sampling, mathematically and in the reality of field experience, will yield comparable results to a complete survey. It remains, however, nothing more than a research tool, albeit a very useful tool, for the collection of detailed information. It offers one of the means for providing the planner with information and assists with the preparation of plans and policies. It is not some kind of magical formula for resolving planning problems.

The use of questionnaires

When the sample for investigation has been selected, the next stage is to approach these units for information. One method is to use a questionnaire, which may be sent out and returned by post. Alternatively the questionnaire may be inserted in a local newspaper or organ of trade circulation, be given to members of a group through their leader (e.g. a study of facilities in rural areas through the regional organization of the Women's Institute or Young

Farmers' Clubs) or may been closed with packaged goods (e.g. in a survey of areas served by a wholesale market). The questionnaire, used in these ways, is undoubtedly the cheapest form of investigation. The cost of postage is negligible compared with interviewers' wages and expenses. The survey is speedier, the administrative work is less, fewer staff are required, and an extensive coverage is possible at a low total cost. Widespread dispersion of the sample presents no problem. From the standpoint of phrasing the questions, the form must be standardized with simple, self-explanatory questions. Ambiguity and vagueness must be avoided. The approach is formal and impersonal so no element of interview bias penetrates either the phrasing of questions or the recording of answers.

On the other hand answers must generally be accepted as final; the questionnaire is inflexible, and no further probing or clarification of a doubtful response is possible. Nor are spontaneous answers possible; each question can be studied by the respondent and a 'correct' answer can be phrased. There is not the depth in penetration of the personal interview. One can collect facts rather than ideas, data rather than experience, and realities rather than thought. The most serious limitation of the questionnaire is however the difficulty of obtaining an adequate response. The response rate is usually far less than interviewing, where personal involvement and rapport between interviewer and interviewee can inspire confidence in the survey. The vital factor is not the decrease in sample numbers, but the strong probability that respondents and non-respondents enjoy different characteristics; in these circumstances deductions based only on the replies received will be biased and the direction of the bias will be unknown. It may be assumed that elderly people who find writing difficult because of physical ailments will not respond, people with strong feelings for or against the subject under investigation will reply, and the better educated may also be more willing to respond.

The element of non-response should be reduced to a minimum by various means. It is axiomatic that the questionnaire should be accompanied by a stamped and addressed envelope. The questionnaire must state categorically that the information is confidential and that the names of respondents will not be disclosed—an index number on each form is sufficient to identify the return and neither name, nor address, nor signature need be asked for. The questionnaire should be accompanied by a brief covering letter, which will arouse an interest in the survey by stating its objects, the name of the organization conducting the investigation, and how the respondent can help. The questionnaire should be short, presented in a pleasing manner and avoid the duplication of questions—to ask both age and date of birth is a common failing, and questions should not be asked when the details are known from the sampling frame. Every question should provide data significant for the problem under investigation.

Non-response will remain despite these precautions. Second, third and fourth copies of the questionnaire can be despatched. If we assume a 40 per cent reply from the first questionnaire, and a further 15 per cent of the total replies to the first reminder, then this latter group should be regarded as more representative of the non-response group than the initial volume of replies and should be weighted-up to 60 per cent in suggesting the overall conclusions. This method is advocated by Moser who suggests 'as an alternative, or supplementary, method; interviewers can be sent to all or some of the non-respondents . . . This procedure will often be ruled out on grounds of expense but is an excellent way of combining the economy of mail questionnaires with the higher response obtained by interviewers.'[11]

Questionnaires have their advantages and have much in their commendation. They attain their greatest response when distributed to the members of a parent organization, when despatched to persons who have been involved in a particular experience, where time or cost is limited, or where the sample is widely dispersed. Its greatest disadvantage is the usually poor rate of return. A major question to be asked before beginning the survey is whether the savings in cost justify this loss in coverage and hence in accuracy.

Interviews

The interview, if properly approached and handled, overcomes this great deficiency of the questionnaire. An almost complete response with some information about those who refuse to co-operate, should be the aim. The sample can be perfect in that any procedure to avoid bias can be strictly adhered to by careful briefing of the interviewers. The personal contact enables the purpose of the survey to be explained fully, vague replies can be elaborated, questions or words can be made intelligible and the language of the survey can be adapted for each individual. Return visits, or a series of surveys in time, are possible. The spontaneous reaction to questions can be noted, and the person who answers the questions can be selected— no control over this factor exists with a questionnaire, which can be completed by any member of the household. Against these advantages must be offset the high costs because of time and travel expenses; an interviewer can distort a response, or intrude his own opinions into the phrasing or emphasis of a question, or the recording of an answer. This element of human fallibility is more probable in the personal contact of interviews than with the formality of the questionnaire, though its disastrous effect on the quality of the investigation can be reduced substantially (if not eliminated) by the method of approach and by the predetermined phrasing of questions.

Many different types of interview are possible. The most frequent is by personal contact, but it can be over the telephone—a method more used in 'telephone-conscious' America than Britain. Nevertheless the cost is less than the personal interview, the method is speedy and refusal rates are low. Interviews may be formal, where the same questions are asked of each person in the same order and using the same words, or informal, where the informant is encouraged to talk under the guidance of a skilled interviewer. Interviews can thus be guided or focused to a greater or lesser extent, and variations in method can take place within the context of each interview. The more formal the interview, the less the skill required of the interviewer, and the more nearly it approaches to the questionnaire.

Informal interviews require the greatest skill. The interviewer projects himself into the interview, which permits greater penetration of attitudes and opinions but makes possible the inclusion of bias. Zweig used this informal approach with great effect. 'A social scientist, especially if he collects his own material, must perform two contradictory mental acts. On the one hand he has to identify himself with the people whom he interviews and describes, to lose his own individuality like an actor . . . and to think entirely on their lines . . . On the other hand he must detach himself from his subject. If you identify yourself . . . your vision becomes narrow, biased and you become too sentimental . . . You need not only identification but also detachment, and the main difficulty is how to combine the two contradictory acts: identification and detachment.'[12]

Interviews also vary substantially according to the type of person being interviewed. There are interviews with experts for technical information or for their professional attitudes. Government inquiries, such as Royal Commissions or the current deliberations about the review of local authority boundaries and functions, normally make use of this method. An interview with an industrialist, the employment exchange manager or the youth employment officer fall within this category and contrast with interviews of people, normally a randomly selected sample at home or at work or during leisure hours, for social facts and attitudes. This latter form of interview may be regarded as the method par excellence of social science. 'After all, what social scientists are interested in are people, and if you want to find out something about a person surely the best way is to ask him.'[13]

Schedules and questionnaires

The logical scientific approach to any interview is to think out in detail beforehand the scope of the questions to be asked. Questions must be phrased to elicit the details about a particular situation and, in the majority of instances, this can best be achieved through listing the questions on a prearranged schedule. This list reminds the researcher of each item, can ensure that questions are asked in a predetermined sequence, secures that the answers are recorded to each question and makes certain that terminology and format are standardized for purposes of comparability. The schedule for use by the interviewer and the questionnaire to be completed by the correspondent thus serve the same general purpose of extending the research worker's powers of observation, though substantial differences in design may occur. The schedule, to be handled only by the interviewers, can be formal, abbreviated and codified; the questionnaire must be complete and self-explanatory. In their design, though no unequivocal rules exist, certain general principles should be observed. These may now be discussed.

The word 'family' is ambiguous. It can mean parents and children; some would include relations living with the unit of marriage; the definition may cover only a person's children; a servant living with the household might be included. This one example will suggest the extreme care which must be taken in the choice of words. People answer a question with the meaning of the words as understood by *them*; this definition need not be the same as the surveyor's interpretation. Also many words with a technical connotation are not understood in this specific sense by the general public; how many persons are aware of the position of administrative boundaries or of their planning implications? Technical words such as region, neighbourhood, precinct, major traffic route, inner area, living room, household, separate accommodation, part-time employment, all have their difficulties of interpretation, and misunderstanding may arise even when the words are defined as in the Census of Population. Phrasing throughout must be simple and unambiguous. This essential characteristic should always be checked by a pilot survey before the main investigation in order to make certain that all questions will be understood by the interviewees in the same way.

Questions should be worded in a concise, natural and conversational manner. 'Do you think . . . ?' is better than 'Do you consider . . . ?'; 'Where do you buy . . . ?' is preferable to 'Where do you purchase . . . ?' Sir Ernest Gowers provides some useful advice on this point.[14] Questions must be specific and precise in order to yield the required information; one would ask 'How many times last week . . . ?' rather than 'How often . . . ?'; figures would be requested rather than percentages; a vague question such as 'Where was your birthplace?' would be better phrased 'In which town or village were you born?' Double-barrelled questions such as 'Were your parents born in this town?' are unsatisfactory and should be asked as two separate questions.

Negative phrasing, 'Don't you think that . . .?, provides an unwelcome form of question in that an answer is implied. Likewise the leading question should be shunned for the question which requires thought and a definite answer: 'Where do you buy your meat?' evokes a positive answer, whereas 'Do you buy your meat at . . .?' can receive a thoughtless reply. Words such as 'normally', 'regularly', 'frequently' must be avoided because of their ambiguity; 'Do you travel regularly to work by train?' should be replaced by 'How often do you travel to work by train?' Hypothetical questions will yield a useless range of replies. 'Would you be willing to pay a reasonable extra rent for . . .?' must be rephrased in the form 'What additional rent would you be willing to pay for . . .?'

On certain difficult or embarrassing questions, an indirect question may yield the more reliable response. Thus religious affiliations can be ascertained through questions about attendance at church or chapel, or whether the children are being educated at a denominational school; the date of birth yields the age of the informant; status and skill at work may be gleaned from questions about the nature of the work performed; the names of schools attended and the dates are better asked for than the quality of education received.

All answers must be recorded as given, and no reliance should be placed on memory. Answers may be recorded verbatim, in essence, or by a mark against a suitable code. All possible answers must be included in this code, or space left for the longest answer if the answers have not been precoded. The distinction between the two types of question, open and closed, is here important. The former provides a greater range of uninhibited response, but is less easy to record; the latter demands that the possible range of answers are known from a pilot study, and also serves to remind the interviewer of the different possible replies. The open question, 'What are your views on . . .?' or 'Which vegetables do you grow in your garden?', contrasts with its closed counterpart, 'Which of the following is most nearly your view on . . .?' or 'Which of the following vegetables . . .?'

The definitions to be used in the field interpretation of data by interviewers (or subsequently in the office) must be consistent.

Certain statistical definitions have been discussed previously, and classifications such as the Standard Industrial and Occupational Classifications can be used with benefit in many inquiries. Some alternative, and additional, definitions used by the Social Survey include:[15]

Household—a group of people living at an address, and who are catered for by the same person. An individual or group of individuals in the same dwelling who have different catering arrangements form a separate household; 'being catered for' is defined as having at least one meal a day when in residence provided by the housewife. Members of the family who live and work away from the home are excluded unless they are children under 16 at a boarding school, fishermen or married persons working away if they return home at least one night a week. Relatives spending four nights a week there, people on holiday and people temporarily in hospital are included.

Employment—persons working more than ten hours a week at the time of the interview are described as 'working'; the 'not working' element consists of retired people and housewives; 'unemployed' includes those who are actively seeking work by being registered at a labour exchange or other employment agency. 'Full-time' work is over 30 hours per week and 'part-time' is over 10 hours per week up to and including 30 hours. People on holiday, strike or away ill are returned as 'working'.

Income—the total amount of money received by the person under consideration from all sources for the last pay week or, for a casual worker, in the seven days before the date of interview. The figure includes bonuses and overtime payments, but excludes family allowances, income tax, health and insurance payments. Money drawn from savings or received in return for board and lodging is excluded.

Questions will be phrased either to elicit factual information (such as age, occupation or the possession of a motor vehicle) or to disclose opinions or attitudes. Though perhaps an obvious point, it should be remembered that the respondent must have enough knowledge or have had the requisite experience for the reply to be valid. A slum-dweller can be invited to talk about the characteristics of his existing environment, and his degree of attachment and attitudes towards moving can be established. To ask about the additional rent which he would be willing to pay for modern accommodation poses a hypothetical question, and the informant's observations on the quality of different layouts would be misleading; this type of question is best asked of comparable families who have moved to a new environment. The results will testify to present reactions to provide an important, but not complete, guide for planning future policy.

On questions of opinion, answers may be difficult to interpret at the analysis stage because the intensity of feeling will vary as between individuals. Attitudes are rarely a straightforward for or against, but include many shades of opinion. On many subjects the informant may wish to express a range of observations, some of which will be positive and others negative. Various rating scales have been devised by which people rate their own attitudes to each question, but these answers have to be combined if the important overall attitude is to be comprehended. To emphasize the answers to questions on one topic alone may be misleading, if other factors are ignored. Social surveys should cover all relevant aspects of a problem, rather than be selective, to overcome this pitfall; and the answers to a series of questions on different topics should be analysed (and presented) as a group rather than singly. Case histories are valuable in this respect.

A further point about attitude questions is the variation of the response in time. Attitudes towards the provision of recreational facilities will vary throughout the seasons, and to a new environment as the families become more settled. As the memories of most people are faulty, the solution is either to spread the interviews of one investigation over a period of months or, preferably, to collect comparable information in a series of sequential studies.

With regard to questions concerned with status or prestige the interviewer must guard against misleading, inaccurate or conventional replies. Such topics include age, income, educational background, occupation and the degree of skill required; the nature of the difficulty will vary as between different social groups. The author's impressions are that people receiving a weekly pay packet are more willing to communicate its contents than the recipients of a monthly cheque; an interviewer is more welcome in a new residential district than in an old locality; he is viewed with less suspicion by local authority tenants than by owner-occupiers.

The placing of 'difficult' questions merits some thought. Easy factual questions should be placed first for several reasons; the respondent may be ill at ease, the interviewer must get the interview going and establish confidence, and the respondent already involved in an interview is more likely to respond to difficult or embarrassing questions after *rapport* has been created. On the other hand the concluding questions should not provide difficulties in response, as the interviewer should depart on a friendly basis rather than abruptly. A further point is that an even flow and continuity of subject-matter should be maintained throughout the schedule; if general and specific questions on the same topic are included, the general question should precede the specific: 'What additional facilities would you like to see in . . .?' should be placed before, and yields a more valuable response than, 'Is a such-and-such facility required?' The arrangement, ordering and sequence of questions are important, and every interview or questionnaire should finish with a genuine thank-you for the person providing the information. The interview is an experience to the respondent and will be discussed with neighbours, colleagues, etc.; the organization conducting the survey will not wish to impair its reputation for its own later research and that of others; thanks are fitting anyway for the time and replies freely given.

Observation

The schedule has provided the scientific method by which consistent data are collected at interviews or through its completion by the person or organization concerned. It must be carefully designed because inaccuracy or bias are all too easy and, in the words of the well-worn cliché, no survey can be better than its questionnaire. The schedule, this time in the guise of field notes, fulfils the same purpose when the survey (in whole or in part) is conducted by observation. The observation and recording of data, the classic and irreplaceable methods of all science, are aided greatly if a list or schedule of required information is provided before the survey. The field note-book should show all those aspects of the survey which require to be observed in the environment of study by listing all appropriate headings. There must be a continual reminder to record what may become self-evident to the trained observer. Casual inspection is not the same as systematic observation and recording which demands the selection of certain data for careful and objective study. Observation is concentrated on the precise terms of reference of the investigation, and the object is viewed accurately and critically. Every item must be fully recorded; reliance should never be placed on memory.

Observation is concerned with conditions at a moment in time, but may involve a sequence of sampling in time as it is difficult to determine the frequency of a particular behaviour by observation alone. It is profitable to record both the observation and the interpretation from the observation; the temptation to record only the interpretation because of its immediate importance is bad research practice and should be avoided, because basic data might be significant for other purposes and may have relationships which are not suspected at the time of collection. Observation offers great advantages when research meets with resistance from the person or group being studied—an industrialist or shopkeeper can refuse an interview; he cannot prevent observation to determine the length of stay of service vehicles, or the number of employees and customers arriving and departing at various times.

Observation can be of many subjects such as the physical potential of land for building purposes, the movement or generation of traffic, or the relationships between the regional pattern of settlement and the physical background. It can take many forms such as using instruments to record information, e.g. traffic counters, a film of the movement of pedestrians in a shopping precinct or a tape-recorder to analyse how planning decisions are reached at a council meeting. Perhaps variants can be introduced into the study, for example studies of pedestrian movement before and after the opening of a new departmental store, or the impact of a bus strike on the volume and mode of travel.

The schedule of information to be observed and noted, whether by interview or by questionnaire or by visual means, must itself be designed and laid out with care. Its function in extending the research worker's accurate powers of scientific observation have been emphasized. When the data has been recorded in as complete a form as possible and checked for omissions and clarity, the schedule must then be used for a variety of analytical purposes. This stage of the research process might include both the coding of detail and its mechanical tabulation. 'Generally speaking, the interviewer is concerned with schedules as a sequence of questions and instructions, the coder with one question through a series of schedules, and the punch operator with the schedule as a series of numbers.'[16] This triple function demands legibility, the avoidance of abbreviations which may not be understood subsequently, and the appreciation throughout that every following stage relies for its validity and usefulness on the accuracy at each of the preceding stages. No alternative to complete accuracy throughout every stage of the investigation can be tolerated or permitted under any circumstances. As the later rectification of omissions and deficiencies is normally impracticable, an undetected error at any stage can destroy the value of a survey. Later, proficiency in the handling of data can never improve upon poor field-work. Time spent on the construction of a schedule will reduce these possibilities of error to the minimum.

Conclusion

Many persons, mistrustful of sampling as some complicated procedure understood only by highly qualified mathematicians, will be encouraged by the words of the head of the statistical department at Rothampsted Experimental Station: 'Fortunately the principles underlying good sampling methods are not unduly difficult to understand, and provided a proper respect is observed for the fundamental rules of procedure I believe they can be successfully applied by those who have statistical experience but who are not primarily mathematical statisticians.'[17] This knowledge is necessary for research workers in planning, if not for all planners. The understanding of environment through sample surveys can contribute much to the advancement of planning thought, and is an aspect of the subject which requires considerable publicity through the medium of ministry handbooks and the work of planning research institutions.

If sampling is regarded as 'difficult', then the opposite tendency to regard questionnaires and interviewing as 'easy' should be discouraged strongly. The construction of a schedule, the precise framing of questions, the sequence of questions at an interview and the exclusion of bias are skilled procedures which require every attention to detail. Certain suggestions can be put forward in a book; the final lessons must be field experience. Examples of the type of information which might be obtained for planning purposes by interview, by questionnaire or by observation will be discussed in the remaining chapters.

1 B. S. Rowntree, *Poverty: a study of town life*, 1902.

2 R. A. Fisher and F. Yates, *Statistical Tables for use in biological, agricultural and medical research*, 1957; M. G. Kendall and B. Babington-Smith, *Tables of Random Sampling Numbers*, Tracts for Computers no. 24, 1939.

3 J. C. Tanner, *Sample Survey of the Road System of Great Britain: Method of Selecting the 1,000 Sample Points*, Road Research Laboratory, Research Note no. RN/3544/JCT, July 1959 (unpublished).

4 M. Young and P. Willmott, *Family and Kinship in East London*, 1957.

5 P. G. Gray, T. Corlett and P. Frankland, *The Register of Electors as a Sampling Frame*, Social Survey, 1950. See also P. G. Gray and T. Corlett, *Sampling for the Social Survey*, vol. A, 1950, pp. 150–206; and L. Moss, *The Scope of Sample Surveys*, Social Survey Paper G 47, 1953.

6 Ministry of Transport, *The Transport of Goods by Road*, H.M.S.O., 1959.

7 F. Yates, *Sampling Methods for Censuses and Surveys*, 3rd ed., 1960, p. 6.

8 References 5 and 7 above, respectively.

9   R. H. Best, *The Major Land Uses of Great Britain*, 1959, ch. 9.

10   B. S. Rowntree, *Poverty and Progress: a second Social Survey of York*, 1941.

11   C. A. Moser, *Survey Methods in Social Investigation*, 1958, pp. 182–3.

12   F. Zweig, *The British Worker*, 1952, p.17.

13   J. Madge, *The Tools of Social Science*, 1953, p. 150.

14   Sir Ernest Gowers, *The Complete Plain Words*, H.M.S.O., 1954.

15   The Social Survey (ed. M. Harris), *A Handbook for Interviewers*, Central Office of Information, 1956, pp. 23–34.

16   D. L. Lamberth, *Schedule Layout*, Social Survey, 1950, p. 7.

17   Yates, op. cit., p. 6.

Note on sampling in Census of Population

A 1 per cent sample was used in the 1951 Census of Population to produce accurate and speedy results for the first tabulations, but the greater volume of information in the county and subject volumes was obtained by processing all schedules. In the 1961 Census of Population only those questions about age, sex, relationship to the head of the family, place of usual residence, place of birth, marital status and children, and details of dwellings, were asked of all persons required to make returns; information was obtained from a 10 per cent sample of the population on occupation, industry, employment, date of last full-time education, qualifications in science or technology*, place of residence on 23rd April 1960 or length of residence at the census address if resident for a year or more*, and particulars of those normally resident but away at census midnight. (New questions*.) Degrees of accuracy are not yet known, but limits of error will be greatest for units such as enumeration districts and small local government districts with a low population.

4

PHYSICAL AND LAND RESOURCE
SURVEYS

PHYSICAL setting, physiographic pattern, geology, mineral resources, landscape characteristics, climatology and the use and
quality of agricultural land will be discussed in this chapter. These
factors may be regarded as the 'physical' or 'natural' elements in
contrast with the 'urban' or 'man-made' characteristics, though the
distinction ignores the fact that the various physical elements in
both town and country would normally be subject to human modi-
fication. The dividing line between the present discussion of 'land
resources' and the inquiries in subsequent chapters must remain
imprecise. The exploitation of minerals depends on accessibility and
the demands of the market, and land fertility may be regarded in
terms both of its economic and physical potential. Any precise
division between the different types of planning survey is also
arbitrary, because a planning appraisal of conditions would examine
all aspects of the environment and perceive the inter-relationships,
present conditions, trends and conditions of the various aspects both
separately and in conjunction with one another. Such studies can be
undertaken at the national, regional, urban, rural and local levels
and, although there are substantial differences both of scale and of
emphasis, surveys within these different areas would employ the
same methods and require an examination of the same coverage of
topics. It is for these reasons that the approach in the subsequent
chapters is by subject, rather than discussing the content of planning
surveys under headings such as village, town, rural, central area and
regional surveys. Planning would use the data collected at these
various levels of operation.

Geographical position

Neither a town nor a region can be regarded as self-contained. Their present problems of land use must be appreciated from the outset as part of a larger physical and social entity with its complex history and geographical evolution revealing an amalgam of local and national forces. For example, the land-use problems of Hereford-shire are attributable at least in part to its position on the Welsh borderland. The evolution of its settlement pattern, its low density of population, the dispersed characteristics of its settlements, the absence of large nucleated villages, and the spacing and size of its market towns cannot be explained only in physical terms of geology, relief, river pattern, water supply or land fertility. Certain special planning problems result such as the difficulties of providing water, electricity and sewerage services to scattered settlements, the provision of a range of modern educational facilities for a sparse rural population and the selection of 'key' or 'focal' villages for development when few rural centres exist.[1]

Milford Haven provides a second illustration of the importance of geographical setting because, as one of Britain's best potential ports with its safe anchorage and deep-water approach, it has long remained virtually undeveloped. The reasons are primarily physical and include the lack of north-south routes in Wales because of the configuration of the land, the fact that there is no populous hinter-land of large industrial towns, and physical distance and inaccessi-bility from the principal British manufacturing centres. The current possibilities of substantial development result from the economic incentive of large oil tankers requiring deep-water berths, and the probability of improved communications by motorways and the Severn Bridge. These changes may overcome physical aloofness.

The Pennine valleys of East Lancashire provide a third example. The essential planning problem focuses on the decline of the cotton industry and the resultant emigration of population. The area expanded rapidly in the nineteenth century because of inherent physical advantages such as soft water for processing, water power and later coal for driving machinery. The significance of a rapid growth within this regional context remains and has provided a legacy of substandard housing, the unsightly scars of derelict land and an insecure economic base. The planning problems of Lancashire in the 1960's obtain directly from the geographical advantages of its position a century previously.

These three examples, so different in their characteristics and land-use problems, emphasize the importance of geographical situation and affinities as an integral and introductory part of any planning study. A ministerial memorandum on the technique of planning survey has made the same point. For county maps a comprehensive introductory chapter should embrace 'the geographical setting of the county; its adjacent authorities and its position in the national communications network'; the corresponding points for town maps are the 'delineation of area with the reasons for the choice of boundaries; position of the town in the region, with neighbouring local authorities and communications . . . description of the physical setting of the town'.[2]

Land-use planning is however concerned with the future. The assessment of physical position will result in an understanding of the changing importance of this setting in time, and will suggest the likely potentialities of the situation for development in the future. Examples of the impact of extra-regional factors on development are numerous. Congestion in Greater London and elsewhere, coupled with a national policy of industrial and population dispersal, has induced the creation of new towns and the expansion of existing towns at substantial distances from the original nucleus. Localities enjoying a nodal situation close to the meeting points of new motorways, or having improved access to a nearby city through the construction of a motorway or the electrification of a railway line, may be expected to change their function, to attract new forms of development and to expand physically. The future of many towns close to the conurbations depends on the position of the regional green belt which, designed to restrict the further lateral growth of the major urban centres and to prevent the coalescence of adjacent towns into one physical unit, will transfer some of the demand for building land from the urban fringe to areas further afield.

The elements of geographical position are dynamic rather than static. Regional patterns and the relative importance of centres have changed in the past, and will change in the future. One factor responsible is increased personal mobility, a second the impact of new communications, a third is the process of industrial growth and decline; a fourth the evolution of society and its changing pressures on individuals and families. These changes are difficult to foresee, but they must be anticipated if land-use planning is to achieve more than the preservation of the *status quo* inherited from past generations.

Surface relief

Detailed contour maps supplemented by field observation will yield much useful detail about the physiographic background of the environment under study, for example the general character of the relief and height of land, the shape and form of hills and valleys, the angle and direction of slopes, river catchment areas and the extent of floodland, the orientation of relief and other physical barriers, the network of the drainage system, and the distribution of lowland and upland. Each item requires careful study, first as a separate factor in its own right for its own importance, and then in its effects upon other physical, human, social and economic factors.

Flooding, height, aspect and slope each influence substantially the use and development of land.[3] Areas liable to flooding may be damp and foggy, but also present construction difficulties; periodic inundations are injurious to foundations, and buildings impede the flow of flood water. Floodland should therefore be avoided by building development, but may be suitable for other functions such as playing fields or grazing land. Drainage authorities have maps showing land eight feet above the highest-known flood level but the data may be inaccurate as the level of floods can vary; local knowledge, the form of the land and the presence of water-loving vegetation can be used to identity the extent of flood areas, and in some places an air photographic cover in time of flood will yield useful information. Localities with a high water table, say within 10 feet of the surface, should also be avoided for settlement.

Excessive height above sea level provides another inhibitive factor to extensive new settlement. An analysis by Sir R. G.

Stapledon, based on agricultural considerations, shows variations from district to district because of local considerations of climate and topography.[4] Somewhere between 1,000 and 1,500 feet there is a 'permanent rigour-of-winter climate line, above which life becomes hard, but not necessarily unbearable, for man and beast'. Conditions remain relatively hard down to a lower level of 700–800 feet. The West Midland Group in their Herefordshire survey have described land above 1,500 feet as 'unsuitable for development', and regard 'development undesirable save in exceptional circumstances' between 800 and 1,500 feet.[5] Considerations of aspect cannot be divorced from height, and there will be lower altitudinal limits on development on slopes facing from north-west to north-east than on those which enjoy the more favourable southerly aspect. There may also be transcending economic or social pressures for development as in the vicinity of limestone workings near Buxton or on the Pennine fringe near Manchester and Sheffield. The amenity advantages of a slope and a view, as at Alderley Edge in North Cheshire, may outweigh other physical disabilities (in this instance a north-facing slope) for private housing development. Planning decisions must ultimately weigh in the balance the importance to be attached to each survey factor operative in the circumstances of any given situation. Any factor may be decisive in certain situations and circumstances, but can be relatively unimportant or insignificant elsewhere. The first tasks of the research worker are to record and to understand those facts that exist; the analysis of their significance will follow.

The importance of degree of slope is also difficult to determine, though its incidence will affect the cost of buildings and their lay-out, the provision of public services, the amount of excavation in road and building construction and the availability of extensive sites. The West Midland Group distinguished between three zones: steeply sloping areas with an approximate average slope of about 1 : 7·5 which they classified as 'unsuitable' for development; areas of moderate slope with inclines of from 1 : 7·5 to 1 : 10 where development was 'undesirable'; and slopes of less than 1 : 10 which were deemed to be 'suitable' for development.[6] Within many towns and residential localities, by contrast, slope may give an area a quality of distinction and so create an element of desirability in an otherwise mundane physical setting.

Geological and mineral surveys

The facts of the geological background should be presented in the introductory sections to regional and urban planning studies, both cartographically in the form of solid and of drift maps and with accompanying descriptions of the principal formations, rock series, soil characteristics, associated vegetational types and other relevant information. This material should then be drawn upon as appropriate in subsequent analyses to assist in explaining salient characteristics in the pattern of settlement, communication routes, the fertility of the land, the exploitation of minerals, relief features, the scenic quality of the environment, the historical process of industrial development, the availability of water resources, and the nature of local building materials. Though an understanding of geological characteristics and of the above relationships may be fundamental to planning thought, and although geological surveys may have to be undertaken for specific planning purposes (e.g. to assess the load-bearing capacity of land or the availability of water resources), their nature and scientific method remain beyond the scope of this book. Geologists are employed as specialists in the Ministry of Housing and Local Government, and in the larger county planning departments with mineral workings and dereliction problems.

Mineral surveys, by contrast, fall wholly within the scope of planning surveys. Extensions to mineral workings, new quarries and mines, tip heaps and the disposal of refuse, and buildings such as crushing plant are subject to planning control. All are included under the heading of 'development' as defined in the Town and Country Planning Act, 1947. To the planner the term 'mineral' covers any rock extracted from mines, quarries or pits which enjoys some commercial value (e.g. limestone, sand, gravel, granite), whereas to a geologist it is the material constituents. The planner requires knowledge about the distribution of all minerals of economic value, and in particular he must be aware of the extent of *workable* deposits so that the natural resources of the country can

be used to the best advantage and not be sterilized from development by other forms of surface land use. If the mineral deposits are
known, then extraction can take place before using the land for
some other form of development; e.g. a hill of glacial sand could be
removed by quarrying and the site then be used for housing, whereas
an earlier use for housing would have prevented the working of this
deposit.

Because of their intrinsic importance to the national economy,
mineral supplies must be safeguarded from surface development for
longer than the 20-year limit of most other provisions in the development plan. Another exception is the reservation of routes for
major highway proposals. The proving of a workable mineral
reserve is a complicated task, involving more than geological considerations. These considerations might include the proximity of
other reserves, their relative quality compared with the local deposit, the present and likely future demand for the product, alternative sources of supply and the possibility of alternative products
to meet the demand. Each factor is difficult to assess, but deposits
may not necessarily be worked even if all these economic requirements are favourable. Further elements such as land ownership, land
availability, situation relative to the market, the cost of transportation, labour supply, the requirements of the operator for a long
tenure of occupation so that the fixed capital invested in plant may
be economic, visual considerations and access to roads or railways
may have to be investigated.

Many sources will have to be consulted to yield the required
information. One-inch drift and solid geological sheets cover most
of the country but rocks are classified by age rather than by their
economic usefulness; the terms used may be misleading, in part at
least: for example, a predominantly limestone series may include
beds of shale or sandstone, and alluvium may contain workable
gravel; the depth of overburden or water conditions may restrict or
even inhibit workability. Certain six-inch geological maps are
published especially for the coal-fields, and others may be consulted
in the office of the Geological Survey. The Memoirs of the Geological Survey are valuable for their district information, bibliographies, and for historical detail about former mineral workings;

they include sheet memoirs which examine the areas of the one-inch geological maps, regional handbooks with general accounts of the principal geological characteristics, and economic memoirs about certain of the rarer mineral resources. Geological literature and libraries must also be consulted.

The operators themselves and their trade organizations are usually helpful, because the preservation of mineral-bearing land is in the interests of both the extractor and the planning authority. Their knowledge may however be more concerned with the business of running a quarry than with the proving of reserves. Field studies, in which aerial photography may have much to contribute, will almost certainly be required; boreholes to indicate the depth of a deposit and laboratory tests to determine its physical composition will require outside consultants.

On existing workings, information will be required about the type of mineral obtained, the methods of extraction, the area with planning approval still to be worked and its estimated life, the markets and use of the mineral, the annual output and trends in production, the nearest comparable source of supply, amount of overburden, the use of machinery and plant, areas used for tipping and tipping requirements, existing and anticipated labour needs, and areas of existing and anticipated subsidence. Planning policy may determine the working programme, or limit the depth of a working, or control tipping, or demand restoration or screening, or require the treatment of derelict land; each form of control demands substantial technical knowledge at the survey stage.

Because of the many national and regional issues involved in mineral extraction, and in view of their land-use responsibilities, the Ministry of Housing and Local Government have undertaken or initiated a substantial number of detailed studies. A memorandum on the Control of Mineral Working was issued in 1951 and revised in 1960, a Technical Memorandum was prepared in 1955, and the Annual Reports contain useful summary details and references to advisory reports such as those on sand and gravel.[7] A series of regional conferences have also been organized by the Ministry to discuss mineral reserves, to examine the planning problems associated with their working, and generally to bring together the planning authorities, the mineral operators and amenity societies. 'The Ministry, in consultation with the Geological Survey and other departments, and with the assistance of the various trade associations, has arranged investigations into most of the minerals produced in England and Wales. The information compiled for the purposes of these investigations is available in the form of memoranda or reports, which have in most cases been discussed at a series of local conferences attended by the local planning authorities concerned and representatives of the industry.'[8] These reports have not been published but should be available within the files of the planning departments concerned.

The Ministry have further suggested that for mineral reserves 'the report of survey should contain a review of the presumed total extent of the mineral field and of the specific areas believed to contain workable minerals, distinguishing wherever possible between *proved* reserves (i.e. proved by test-boring or other means), *probable* reserves (i.e. where this is good reason to believe in the presence of economically workable minerals) and *possible* reserves (i.e. areas where there is merely geological evidence that a mineral may occur in workable quantity and quality, but proof depends on further exploration); and distinguishing also land which is known to be under the control of a mineral operator, i.e. owned, leased or under option'.[9]

Brief mention should also be made of geological surveys to indicate water resources. There may be large-scale underground water supplies in pervious rocks such as chalk, and reservoirs can be constructed in incised valley areas of high regular rainfall on impervious strata. Water-gathering grounds, feeding either surface reservoirs or underground supplies, must be delineated and protected from development likely to cause pollution. The extent of a gravel deposit, offering both a dry site above flood level and potable water at the base, may determine the desirable limits for a settlement's physical expansion. The availability of local water supplies may prove to be one of the decisive factors in determining the location of new small settlements or sites suitable for the expansion of industry.

Surveys of landscape quality

The quality of the landscape also depends in part upon geological factors. An assessment of its quality by local planning authorities becomes important so that relative degrees of stringency in development control can be exercised in the various areas. No precise or scientific measuring rod is possible, and much will depend on local circumstances—a small wooded glen within an industrial town enjoys greater visual importance than a similar woodland in the Welsh border country. The delimitation of areas in various categories should be undertaken in conjunction with local field, amenity and preservation societies, and conferences can usefully be arranged to discuss the effective degrees of planning control in each locality. They serve the dual purpose of obtaining information and 'putting over' planning policies.

Many possible classifications of landscape quality exist. The West Midland Group, for example, have suggested three zones.[10] Zone I included 'areas of great natural beauty in which no non-agricultural development and no future quarrying should be permitted' and 'areas which, because of their proximity to urban areas, have particular recreational value quite apart from any landscape beauties they may possess'. It was thought that land in these zones should generally be in public ownership or trust and available for public enjoyment. Zone I would include attractive and dominant skylines, frequented commons, hills and woods near towns, wild life and nature reserves, major areas of attractive coastal scenery, notable beauty spots and the major English homes and landscaped gardens.

Zone II included 'areas of natural beauty in which industrial and housing development should be permitted only when such development is in the best interests of agriculture, to provide the extended services required in all rural areas, and for the extraction of minerals'. Within this zone 'building and quarrying should be permitted only under strict control so that the form and character of the landscape is not impaired'. The areas will be more extensive than in Zone I. The approach is not 'preservation' but an appreciation of the fact that the scenic quality depends very much on the activities of rural life, supplemented by the careful selection and development of sites in the greater interests of the area. Zone III enjoys a lower amenity status and was described as 'areas of natural beauty where some new development, either industrial or housing, may be of value, both nationally and locally, but from which noxious or undesirable industries should be excluded'.

To these landscape divisions must be added those urban or village areas of particular charm or beauty because of their lay-out, the grouping of buildings, historical associations or building materials. Again, degrees of planning decision and control require to be formulated to retain and to enhance this valuable element of the national heritage. Also to be included would be those designated (or proposed) areas such as national parks, nature reserves, areas of outstanding natural beauty, long-distance footpaths, tree-preservation orders, National Trust holdings, access agreements to open country, green belts and other localities where landscape quality must receive high recognition. In addition, classifications of landscape scale, texture, colour and materials would assist materially in design control.

Surveys of climate and atmospheric pollution

Climatology, like geology, exists as a discipline in its own right with its body of literature and history of scientific method. Its specialized findings have to be interpreted in their impact and potentialities for the use and development of land by planners. The subject has received incidental mention previously with reference to aspect in relation to height, to the mists of low-lying lands and to seasonal rainfall as a factor in the siting of reservoirs. It influences the types of agricultural production, and hence the pattern of rural land use. Factors such as aspect, shelter, insulation, precipitation, liability to frost and length of the growing season may have to be studied. New settlement should avoid frost pockets, northern aspects and the floors of deep valleys with their limited sunlight; the direction of the prevailing wind provides one factor in the siting of noxious industry, including sewage works; an optimum policy for land use, e.g. for areas of afforestation, can be prepared only in the

light of detailed climatological knowledge relative to the requirements of specific crops. The *Climatological Atlas of the British Isles*
is arranged in sections covering pressure, wind, temperature, rainfall, snow, thunder, humidity, sunshine, fog and visibility and cloud
to provide a valuable introductory source,[11] and regional studies
appear in the British Association handbooks.[12] Queries about the
availability of local data can be addressed to the Meteorological
Office. The most comprehensive textbook is by R. Geiger[13] and, in
each of the above instances, the extensive bibliographies will lead
the research worker to further published material.

The investigation of local climatic factors should form an
essential part of the preliminary survey of an area. Places only a few
hundred feet apart may have radically different climates as a result
of differences in elevation, topography (which influences air drainage, wind force and wind direction), soil and vegetation or any
combination of such differences. Pollutants aggravate the climatic
differences and may influence the planning of a rural land-use
pattern. Of great human significance is their correlation with health
factors, especially the incidence of bronchitis. 'A study of the
general pattern of death rates in Lancashire indicates that south-
easterly districts of the county have the highest death rates. These
districts have the most adverse climatic conditions, coupled with a
high degree of air pollution from both local and distant sources.
Superimposed upon this general climatic-health pattern is the
topographical factor that the settlements in valley locations are, in
general, unhealthy. Valleys forming the site of urban development
(with or without associated industrial development) are highly
suspect, but open locations, even where sea mists and fogs occur,
are in general relatively healthy areas.'[14]

Data of this character should provide an important element in
the development decision, and Howes has suggested for consideration the calculation of a 'site occupation factor'. This measuring
index would permit 'a numerical estimate of the relative importance
of various land uses, in order to secure the fullest benefit from the
healthiest sites and the avoidance of the worst sites for intense
uses . . . The factor . . . is the total amount of time spent upon a
given site by all the occupants concerned, when calculated for

different land use purposes'.[15] The argument that the healthiest sites should be reserved for the most intensive use is logical from this climatic-health standpoint; in view of planning's emergence through the public-health legislation of the nineteenth century, this factor requires greater consideration in planning decisions. Planning authorities may be able to undertake the various surveys; if not, professional advice should be obtained.

Control over atmospheric pollution is divided: the Clean Air Act 1956 placed the establishment of smoke control areas and control over the height of new industrial chimneys on local authorities; the siting of industry and the relationships between different uses are functions of the local planning authorities. Ziebicki has argued that 'for an air-pollution map for planning purposes it is not sufficient to show the bulk of impurities suspended in the area or deposited on the ground . . . but it is essential to show the estimated areas which are liable to various degrees of contamination from particular sources of pollution under the most unfavourable weather conditions likely to occur'.[16] This form of map, whether of conditions at the time of survey, or under different wind or other climatic circumstances, or averages over a period of years, will be valuable to all concerned with the problem. It gains significantly when the data from actual measurements is supplemented by the location on ordnance maps of likely sources of pollution, including factory chimneys and residential areas of varying density not subject to smoke control.

Supplementary information, obtained by direct inquiry, should include the type of fuel used, the amount of fuel burned daily with seasonal variations, the velocity of draught, number of chimneys and their height and diameter, cowls and other distributing devices, the height of the factory buildings, type of combustion appliances and method of operation, the presence of grit arrestors and their performance, substances emitted in addition to the usual pollutants and their importance, and any special requirements for a particular industrial process. This information will require specialized knowledge for its interpretation, but when 'properly related to the distribution of the winds at various velocities, will enable the approximate values of the ground-level concentration of pollution from individual chimneys at various points within their range to be calculated'.[17] With the facts known and presented in an intelligible manner, planning policy may now be devised.

Planning surveys must also investigate the impact of planning decisions, for instance about the spatial distribution of uses or the pattern of buildings or a screen of trees, on micro-climate. Can sound from an aerodrome or the spread of chimney effluent be cushioned to leeward by a belt of trees? What variations exist between the effectiveness of different species of trees through differences in height, amount of foliage and its seasonal length of leaf coverage to stop noise or pollution carried by winds? How can the buildings around a shopping centre or pedestrian precinct best be grouped to provide the most agreeable or least unpleasant climatic conditions, to reduce exposure from strong winds, and to make the most of the sun? Shelter-belts might be planted to protect exposed playing fields or elevated housing sites: 'a shelter belt only 20 feet high will give quite effective protection if sited as far as 120 feet from a one-storey building, and when the trees reach their full height they should, if well designed, give full protection at this distance'.[18] The preliminary surveys would include work on the directions from which the local prevailing and cold winds, and driving rain and snow, are likely to come. A further consideration, which again demands climatological knowledge, is that a belt of contour planting on a slope may impede the downward drainage of cold air.

The evidence from the London climatological survey may prove valuable in appreciating the effect of buildings on climate. The main emphasis of this work is on understanding London's heat island, a body of warm air which commonly lies within and above the city. A close network of climatological stations has been established in the urban area, and traverses in a vehicle equipped to record temperature and humidity changes are also being used.[19]

In considering this variety of possible climatic surveys, it will have become obvious that 'some knowledge of the elements of meteorology is necessary for the town and country planner, if only to indicate to him where he must be prepared to consult the experts'.[20] This sound advice has a wider application; it is true for all research studies. Research workers must be aware of their own limitations both in knowledge and in techniques of investigation; an incompetent survey may be more misleading than the previous lack of knowledge.

The use and quality of agricultural land

Many official pronouncements exist about the planning attitude towards agricultural land. 'One of the main objects of planning policy is to ensure that productive agricultural land is not taken for development where less good land would serve the same purpose . . . The plan must, therefore, be based on a real appreciation of agricultural needs, including the relative agricultural value of land in a locality.'[21] The point at issue for the research worker is the difficulty of providing the initial information. What precisely is 'productive agricultural land'? How can one assess 'the relative agricultural value of land' in several different localities as the prelude to steering development from A to B?

Geological maps, and especially those depicting the superficial deposits rather than the solid formations, make some initial contribution to the complex assessment. The Soil Survey of Great Britain is proceeding steadily, but the date for its completion is unknown and certainly distant. The detailed mapping is at the scale of six inches to one mile, with publication at the one-inch scale over O.S. base maps and with accompanying memoirs. In addition, certain special surveys have been undertaken for local planning authorities, e.g. Lancashire. The most recent position is described in the annual reports.[22] The lack of a complete national soil survey is a severe deficiency when planners are concerned with the location of new settlements or directing the expansion of existing centres of population. The natural resources of the country, in this as in several other respects, remain unknown.

Apart from the published ordnance survey maps, which might be used to interpret relief characteristics and the distribution of broad vegetational types such as woods, parkland, orchards and moorland, there was nothing until the 1930's to provide precise information on the land use and state of cultivation over most of

Great Britain. The Land Utilization Survey of Great Britain then mapped land use at the 1 : 63,360 scale over the fourth or popular edition for the whole country, and distinguished arable land, meadowland and permanent pasture, heathland and moorland, woodland, houses with gardens, orchards, nurseries and land which was agriculturally unproductive.[23] The data relate generally to the years 1930–5. The distribution maps are supplemented by county reports, which provide a valuable background to the study of an area and to the varying characteristics of its different parts. They are introduced by a description of the physical background of the county with diagrams of relief, drainage, geology and soils. A description of the pattern of land use at the date of survey follows, with each category of use being analysed separately and related to crops, stock and types of farming. The county is then divided into land-use regions with each area being described, and an historical section examines the evolution of the land-use and settlement patterns. Many of the written analyses which accompanied the development plans of county planning authorities in 1951 owe a debt of gratitude to these pioneer publications of great geographical merit.

The results have been presented on the 'land utilization' map of the National Planning series of maps at the scale of 1 : 625,000. At this scale, generalizations are inevitable and 100 acres is the smallest area which can be distinguished. This information on land use is supplemented by a 'Types of Farming' map at the same scale. The main pasture, intermediate and arable types of farms are classified into 17 subdivisions. This latter document was prepared by the economics branch of the Ministry of Agriculture and was completed in 1939. Its principles of classification are threefold—the proportion of arable land on each farm, the dominant form of enterprise and, for mixed farming, a minimum requirement of eight separate enterprises including both livestock and crops was stipulated.

A third map in this national series, 'The Grasslands of England and Wales', 'relates to conditions before the wartime campaign for the ploughing up of permanent grassland, but this in no way invalidates the map as a general pointer towards the various qualities of grassland or as a general guide to land-use policy. The map is an attempt to classify on a floristic basis the permanent grasslands of England and Wales; rough and hill grazings are included and the the distribution of the various types of grassland is distinguished.'[24]

Planning authorities however require something more than geology, land use, grassland and types of farming maps. Land classification, based on detailed studies and national in their scope, is necessary.[25] A map with this title in the National Planning series resulted from the Land Utilization Survey and distinguishes three major categories. Subgroups 1–4 comprise major category I, good-quality land, which is 'highly productive when under good management'. Land in this category enjoys site conditions which are not too elevated, level, gently sloping or undulating, and of favourable aspect; the soil is deep, has favourable water conditions and the texture, mostly loams, may include some peats, sands, silts and clays. Major category II, medium-quality land, with two subgroups, is 'land of only medium productivity even when under good management. Productivity is limited by reasons of the unfavourable operation of one or more of the factors of site or soil character, e.g. by reason of high elevation, steepness of site, unfavourable aspect, shallowness of soil, or defective water conditions.' The four subgroups of major category III, poor-quality land, cover 'land whose productivity is low by reason of the extreme operation of one or more factors of site and soil'.

This classification is primarily physical, and significant differences may be concealed by the small scale of the presentation. Human considerations, both economic and historical, will also operate. Accessibility, in the local sense of distance from the nearest road and regionally relative to the consumer markets, will influence the choice of crop; the quantity and quality of local water supplies will affect the suitability of a farm for stock; drainage can be improved by deeper cultivation; the continuation of upland and marginal farms in production may depend on demand or the amount of subsidy. These factors are more difficult to map objectively than the purely physical elements, though they are revealed to a limited extent by the interpretation of grassland, land use and types of farming maps.

These sources of information are about to be supplemented by the new land-use survey of Great Britain.[26] The relatively simple seven-category basis of the 1930 land-use survey has been replaced by 52 separate categories of land use to provide a greater differentiation of crops and other types of land use. This survey is on the six-inch scale as previously, but the results are to be published on 865 maps at 1:25,000 (two-and-a-half-inch scale). The major categories, each with subdivisions, include settlement, industry, transport, derelict land, open space, grassland, arable land, market gardening, orchards, woodland, heathland, moorland and rough land, water and marsh, and unvegetated land.

A logical sequence in survey investigation begins with the land characteristics and leads to the farm and farming units. Details of farm boundaries may be obtained by planning authorities from the regional offices of the Ministry of Agriculture, though the information is confidential and should not be published. When mapping this data isolated fields should be linked to the main farm unit, and the position of the main buildings and of access points should be shown clearly. Before taking land from a farming unit for development, the effects on the economy of the farm must be understood. The economy can be jeopardized if the site forms a large proportion of the total farm area, if the unit is small and the fixed costs of the farm have to be carried by the output from the remaining acres, if the loss of land prevents access to further fields, or if the land is a particular type essential to the functioning of the farm economy and limited in area on the farm. One field may be essential to the functioning of a farm. On the urban-rural fringe, in villages, and elsewhere in rural areas understanding of the farm economy by local investigation should provide an essential prerequisite to planned development.

Detail about the size and layout (e.g. fragmentation) of farm holdings will also yield pertinent planning information and may suggest the need for the amalgamation of units, the consolidation of farms and generally for a positive approach to rural land-use planning in the national interest to make the best use of available resources. Thus on the fertile acres of Herefordshire, 44 per cent of the total number of farms are units of less than 20 acres in extent.

'Few of these holdings reach the level of production which has been achieved on the bigger farms, since the occupiers possess few implements and cannot undertake any arable cultivation without help . . . In a country where agricultural land is so limited in area, the existence of so many holdings of this type is a serious problem.' The resultant recommendation is that 'the number of farms in the "under 20 acres" group should be reduced, except in market-gardening districts, since this type of holding can rarely be an efficient economic unit'.[27] Planning policy has emerged from the content of factual surveys, but unfortunately there is as yet no mechanism for the implementation of these particular land-use objectives.

Studies of farm boundaries and sizes should be followed by surveys of agricultural productivity. The ensuing comments summarize the methods of approach which might be used to assess the loss to the community of 10 acres of farmland.[28] This could be described as the loss of 10 acres of land of a particular quality, but the effective loss is the support of a number of cows or the acreage of wheat which could perhaps be translated into so many gallons of milk or bushels of grain. The reference is to gross output, i.e. the monetary value of the produce at its current wholesale price, though net output provides the more appropriate figure. Net output is gross output less the input for the purchase of livestock, feeding stuffs, implements, seeds, etc., and provides the most useful measure of productivity. Details of net output are calculated for different types of farms by the Ministry of Agriculture, and appear in *Farm Incomes in England and Wales*. To be offset against this figure of net loss must be the gain from the new use of the land which, if under housing, will depend on the size of the plot and the value of its produce.

If two or more sites are competing for development, then three sets of factors are involved in the analysis:

1. The comparative net outputs from the different areas must be assessed as described, either in general terms from the reports on farm incomes or in detail with the assistance of an agricultural economist. The general terms would be adequate for the relative consideration of two new town sites, whereas

more detail would be relevant for smaller acreas of potential development.

2. The relative costs of developing the two sites must then be assessed. Many considerations exist and their cost will vary from site to site, but clearance, levelling, excavation, provision of public services, road construction and house foundations should each be considered.

3. The extra costs of developing the poorer site must then be compared with the gain to the nation of leaving the better site under its agricultural use. This method was applied by Dr Wibberley in his evidence on the use of Lymm or Mobberley as a site for a New Town for overspill from Manchester.[29] His conclusion was that the net farm income capitalized in perpetuity at $3\frac{1}{2}$ per cent resulted in £835,000 at Lymm compared with £576,000 at Mobberley; therefore an additional expenditure of £259,000 would be justified at Mobberley to safeguard the land at Lymm, or £835,000 could be spent on higher densities in Manchester as an alternative to development on agricultural land at Lymm.

These arguments show how agricultural productivity can be measured and used in the planning process. Useful as these assessments are, they represent only a part of the greater whole—the measurement of the overall cost benefit analysis which should be undertaken before development is decided. There are other social and economic costs and benefits which provide part of the equation, and which should be included within the Development Balance Sheet suggested by Dr Lichfield and to be discussed in the final chapter. The present discussion has been concerned primarily with the physical and directly observable elements of the situation, rather than with the total planning assessment.

Forestry may be regarded as a specialized form of agricultural land use, in that trees are essentially a crop with a sequence of planting, growth and felling. Because of their semi-permament nature and their aesthetic significance, the felling of trees is subject to control by local planning authorities, though planting proposals are not shown on Development Plans. Surveys thus become necessary to permit this control to be exercised without detriment either to local amenity or to the sequence of forestry operations. The first stage of the investigation should be to map all woodlands and groups of trees, distinguishing between three separate groups of factors for each woodland area—the type of trees, and their age, height and economic importance as a timber crop; the amenity, visual, recreational and scientific significance and quality of the sites (or parts thereof) under consideration; and the nature of the ownership, particularly areas of well-managed woodland owned either by the Forestry Commission or subject to a dedication covenant. Some woodland areas may require rehabilitation, including the clearance of scrub woodland and its replanting under trees of economic importance. Elsewhere a policy of afforestation might be appropriate, which would involve the study of land ownership and of geological, soil and climatic features in areas suitable for planting, and the selection of suitable tree species. In other localities tree planting may be desirable for amenity purposes, for example in conjunction with mineral workings or the routes of new highways. These considerations may devolve upon the research worker in the smaller planning authorities or, in the larger administrative units, on the landscape designer. The subject-matter is specialized and, in the more penetrating studies, outside advice may be desirable.

Conclusion

Physical surveys provide the basis for understanding many planning problems at village, urban and regional levels of appreciation. Any factor may operate in the area under study, but its significance can vary in different locations. Thus the extent of floodland may be decisive in determining the extent of a small town or village expansion; in a conurbation with a gross shortage of building land, it may necessitate either extensive drainage or raising the land by tipping to facilitate development. Although the physical factor remains the same, the planning solutions differ greatly because every land-use situation involves a complex amalgam of physical and other elements. The inherent danger of approaching the content of planning surveys subject by subject is that the inter-relationships between diverse subjects may be forgotten, and any one topic may receive undue attention. Planning surveys should be comprehensive if all factors operative in the environment under study are to be seen in their true relationships.

1   West Midland Group, *English County: A Planning Survey of Hereford-shire*, 1946; A. R. Duncan, *Herefordshire: County Survey and Analysis*, County Planning Department, 1951.

2   Ministry of Housing and Local Government, *General Survey of the Area and its Problems*, Technical Memorandum no. 1, 1955, pp. 1–2 (unpublished).

3   See L. Keeble, *Principles and Practice of Town and Country Planning*, Estates Gazette, 1959, chs. 5 and 8, for a useful discussion of these and other survey factors.

4   Sir R. G. Stapledon, *The Land: Now and Tomorrow*, 1935, pp. 94–5.

5   West Midland Group, op. cit., p.19.

6   West Midland Group, ibid., p. 21.

7   Ministry of Housing and Local Government, *The Control of Mineral Working*, H.M.S.O., 1960; Ministry of Housing and Local Government, *Mineral Working*, Technical Memorandum no. 3, 1955 (unpublished); Ministry of Housing and Local Government, *Annual Reports*, H.M.S.O.

8   Technical Memorandum no. 3, ibid., p. 5.

9   Technical Memorandum no. 3, ibid., p. 6.

10   West Midland Group, op. cit., pp. 44–5, 48.

11   Air Ministry, *Climatological Atlas of the British Isles*, H.M.S.O., 1952.

12   e.g. A. Garnett, 'Climate' in British Association, *Sheffield and its Region*, 1956, pp. 44–69.

13   R. Geiger, *The Climate near the Ground*, 1957.

14   G. Howes, *Location, Health and Planning*, 1960, p. 34 (unpublished Diploma thesis in the Library of the Town and Country Planning School, University of Manchester).

15   Howes, ibid., p.86.

16   J. I. Ziebicki, *Noxious Industry in Town*, 1959, p. 40 (unpublished Diploma thesis in the Library of the Town and Country Planning School, University of Manchester).

17   Ziebicki, ibid., p.18.

18 Ministry of Agriculture, *Shelter Belts for Farmland*, H.M.S.O., 1961, p. 8.

19 I am indebted to Dr T. J. Chandler of the Department of Geography, University College, London, for this brief statement. See *Weather*, June 1960, and *Geography*, November 1961, for some early results of this survey.

20 E. G. R. Taylor, 'Climate in Relation to Planning' in Association for Planning and Regional Reconstruction, *Town and Country Planning Textbook*, 1950, p. 14.

21 Ministry of Town and Country Planning, Circular 99, *Safeguarding of Agricultural Land*, 1950. See also Circular 43/58 of the Ministry of Housing and Local Government.

22 Agricultural Research Council, Soil Survey Research Board, *Soil Survey of Great Britain*, H.M.S.O. (e.g. Report no. 12, 1959.)

23 L. D. Stamp, *The Land of Britain: its use and misuse*, 1950.

24 Planning Maps, Explanatory Text no. 5. Vegetation: *the Grasslands of England and Wales*, Ordnance Survey, 1952, p. 1.

25 See L. D. Stamp, *Fertility, Productivity and Classification of Land in England and Wales*, 1941. Also West Midland Group, *Land Classification in the West Midland Region*, 1947.

26 A. Coleman and K. R. A. Maggs, *Land-Use Survey Handbook*, Isle of Thanet Geographical Association, 1960.

27 West Midland Group, *English County*, op. cit., pp. 102–3, 105.

28 See, for example, N. Lichfield, 'Economics of Planned Development', *Estates Gazette*, 1956, chs, 18–19; J. T. Ward, 'The Siting of Urban Development on Agricultural Land', *Journal of Agricultural Economics*, December 1957, pp. 451–66.

29 G. P. Wibberley, *Agriculture and Urban Growth*, 1959, ch. 5. For the impact of location on rural land use see M. Chisholm, *Rural Settlement and Land Use*, 1962.

5

LAND USE AND BUILDING SURVEYS

AS PLANNING is concerned with the use and development of land, studies of the existing pattern of land use are fundamental to the subject. The approach, initially, should be to appreciate the present distribution of land uses as a product of the past growth, history and present activities of an area. The resultant pattern will not necessarily be efficient either in whole or in part, but must provide the starting point for any form of future plan or proposal. An intimate knowledge of the composition of an area provides the essential prerequisite to rational planning. The need is to understand the existing distribution and structure of land uses, their land and building needs, and the trends of land-use development. In the words of a ministerial circular, 'physical planning must be based on an accurate knowledge of existing land use. Maps should therefore be prepared showing the predominant uses of all land in the planning area, and a record of all major changes should be maintained.'[1] In practice the statutory requirements are insufficient to yield other than the barest minimum of information, and much further information is often required as will be suggested.

Land use within its historical context

A land-use survey is concerned with the surface utilization of all developed and vacant land at a specific point in time in a given area. These data are not fixed or unalterable. Land use changes to meet new ways and conditions of life. Buildings designed for a particular use become obsolete, but may attract new uses within the old fabric. The demand for new uses of land may be inspired by technological change, and will vary as the community changes in its size and composition or in its requirements; expansion may be lateral or vertical, or within the same unit by changes in the density of occupation; some changes are short-lived, whereas others represent a more constant demand.

An understanding of these dynamic qualities in land use will emerge from an historical assessment to reveal the successive phases of physical development. The selection of time intervals will depend on the availability of old maps and other historical evidence, and on the periods of development and stagnation which were significant for the town under study. There are two different types of presentation: a composite map would show the extent of the present physical development and the areas developed during different historical periods, and detailed maps would depict the building pattern and road lay-out of the town at pertinent dates in the past. The latter maps are easier to interpret when drawn to a consistent scale and orientation, and when data about former land uses from the evidence of commercial and street directories are superimposed over the then street and building patterns. Sources of information and the limitations of their accuracy should always be stated on every map.

The interpretation of the changing form of land use will involve an appreciation of physical background factors and the growth to importance of an urban area at the local and regional levels of appreciation. The concern will be with factors of location such as the initial site conditions and with the granting of rights and privileges. Towns with strong historical traditions and attributes may merit more comprehensive treatment but, in general, the function of the historical account in a planning survey is to introduce and to see in their perspective the old and modern features of the town at the date of survey. Present-day planning is concerned with a short, albeit important, span in the life-cycle of an environment. This thought, rather humbling in its implications, demands knowledge of the larger time processes. The town is as it is because it was as it was, and changing economic and social circumstances result in changed land-use patterns, and changes in function requiring new physical elements. This is the background to which planners are contributing. 'We must not too simply begin . . . with

fundamentals as of communications . . . but above all things seek
to enter into the spirit of our city, its historic essence and continuous
life. Our design will thus express, stimulate and develop its highest
possibility, and so deal all the more effectively with its material and
fundamental needs.'[2]

Against this background of the historical emergence of the
present land-use characterisics may be seen the introduction of
industry or of new forms of communication and their impact on
the growth, form and quality of the environment. These changes
did not finish when the counties and county boroughs made their
surveys of land use for the 1951 Development Plans. The concept
of an ever-changing and dynamic sequence of land use should
provide the basis for planned action, and an important requirement
in the first review of approved Development Plans is to 'compare
the extent and pattern of changes since the first survey'.[3] The history
of land use is continuous; it does not exist in isolation but results
from, and summarizes, the interaction of operative economic, social
and physical phenomena within an environment.

The land-use map

Presentation can either place all uses in juxtaposition on the same
map, or each use can be placed on a separate map. The composite
map is usually preferred as it provides an immediate impression of
the principal land uses, the pattern of use, the major functions of
each locality, the contrast between different sections of the survey
area and the intermingling of uses. Separate maps may however be
designed to single out for study the distribution of one characteristic, and are most relevant when a subject such as industrial location or the distribution of public open space rather than an area is
under examination. The usefulness of these maps will diminish with
time. A land-use survey requires to be kept up-to-date, and periodic
revision must be undertaken. A re-survey has to be made at regular
intervals. Alternatively, a record can be maintained of changing
uses through the approval of planning permissions or through the
rating office, although both methods should be supplemented by
field checks as neither provides a complete coverage of changes in

land use. Systems to record this changing use of land as part of a continuous planning process have been designed by local planning authorities and have been discussed in the *Journal of the Town Planning Institute*.[4]

Because of the great significance attached to land-use maps in planning, much thought and study must underlie the system of classification. The standard system evolved by the Ministry of Town and Country Planning has much to commend it.[5] The maps can be understood by planners and the public without having to 'learn' a new notation before they can read each map; the content may be compared as between different localities; there is a national base for a systematic study of the characteristics and trends of the urban and county environments. These advantages of national uniformity are considerable, but other and more meaningful classifications are possible. Undue reliance on this one approach may obscure pertinent local details or result in an inadequate appraisal of land-use characteristics.

The conventional classification and recording of the use of land is by its functional activity, i.e. the use by which it fulfils its purpose. A simple or small-scale land-use map would distinguish only between the major land uses such as residential, industrial or commercial. As the scale of the map is enlarged, areas with these predominant uses may be further subdivided as required until the individual use of each building and plot of land can be shown. At the larger scales, in town centres for example, it will be necessary to record the uses on each floor of every building. In other words, the larger the scale of the map, the greater the range of detail which can be recorded, and the greater the flexibility of the classification system; the smaller the scale, the more generalized must be the functional land-use pattern which is revealed.

The mapping of data, so far, has been by function. Different forms of classification and grouping may however be necessary so that a range of uses can be analysed as a related group. For example, it may be necessary to examine the land uses which serve a region, or which are related to a traffic artery, or which serve a particular section of the community, or which are linked with an industrial activity. This association between land uses is not the same as the spatial distribution of land uses in a locality—the content of a land-use survey—but the subgroups of a land-use survey must be capable of being classified into a variety of these analytical categories. These later considerations of the research process must be taken fully into account when designing the preliminary stages of the investigation.

Quite apart from the collection and recording of data to permit both the functional and the analytical grouping of related uses, the contents of a land-use survey should be presented in the form of statistical summaries to reveal the area under each category of use in acres, the proportion of *all* land under each use and the proportion of *developed* land under each use. Various ratios may be valid such as the relationships between land use and population size, or land use and the density of physical development. Such tabulations clarify complex data, assist in the interpretation of relationships and permit comparisons between the conditions in different areas.

Some complexities of detailed land-use surveys

The normal principles of statistical classification are that each unit can be placed in only one category and the categories should be derived from one principle of classification. This desirable scientific method cannot always be followed in land-use surveys. The guiding principle should be the use of a building or an area of land, but difficulties arise in practice when a variety of different uses occur on a site under the same ownership or occupancy. For example, an industrial enterprise may have workrooms, outdoor storage space, packing warehouse, an office block, paint store, car-parking lots, amenity area and playing fields. As these activities can be regarded as ancillary to the industrial activity it may be appropriate to present this varied range of different uses under a generalized industrial heading at the one-inch scale. Even so, difficulties arise. There is a tendency to show a small playing field within the curtilage of an industrial establishment as 'predominantly industrial', whereas the same area of land separated from the firm and situated in a rural area woud tend to be classified to 'open space'. The land-*use* function, in each instance, is the same. At the larger scales every separate use should be distinguished. A land-use map is not a map of land ownership or land occupancy.

Complications now arise when multiple uses occur on the same plot of land or within the same building. A use may change with depth away from a street frontage as when a shop has workrooms, storerooms or residential accommodation to the rear. A use may change with height, e.g. when a ground-floor shop is succeeded by two floors of offices, when communal services are located on the ground floor of a block of residential flats, or when car parking is provided in the basement. In these examples the uses may be inter-connected or associated, either horizontally or vertically, or the different uses may function in their own right as separate entities. For example, the basement car park, surface shops and offices above may operate under the same ownership and function as ancillary activities of a retail business; alternatively, there need be neither physical nor managerial connection, and each land use could operate with its own separate access and other service facilities. These distinctions require to be appreciated, if the pattern of land uses and the number of different uses in an area are to be understood.

The cartographic recording and presentation of such multiple uses is no easy task. Symbols can be used to indicate the predominant use on each floor, with horizontal and vertical links to connect associated land uses with their major functional activity. Overlays permit the precise position of the different uses at each level to be recorded, and the notation can indicate when connections exist between adjacent land uses either above, below or sideways—but the reading of a series of overlays as one unit is not easy. The presence of basements increases the problems of mapping; they may, for example, underlie adjacent streets and how is the basement 'overlay' related to a base map of ground-floor site areas and land uses? The preparation of 'land-use cross-sections' through the more complicated localities will help to clarify these detailed land-use maps. The statistical tabulation of land-use areas and their uses at each floor level is an easier exercise.

A plot of land may enjoy a dual use, often in conjunction with agriculture, such as rough grazing and a playing field, water gathering ground and afforestation area, or service training ground and hill pasture. Comparable uses should be distinguished according to their differences in accessibility, such as a public playing field available to all groups of the population in contrast with a site reserved for use by certain age groups or available at certain hours or in certain seasons only; restrictions on the use of a public hall may limit its use by the community. Similar functions can impose very different land-use needs. For instance, the policy of local authorities towards public access in water catchment areas varies greatly; another illustration is that docks are used for different purposes and there is a little similarity between the associated land-use requirements of, say, fish, fruit and timber docks. Each of these various uses and their implications should be recorded; a generalization or a distinction between outwardly comparable uses can be made later as appropriate. If the generalization is made at the time of the field survey then significant facts may be withheld from later analysis. The concept of a 'predominant use' can be a dangerous over-simplification of a complex intermixture which should be understood both on the basis of its various components and as an entity.

More than observation is required to appreciate the complexity of uses. Visual inspection from the street will not reveal the use of upper storeys and basements in a central area, similar external façades can conceal differences in back development, and large sites may not be visible in their entirety. Multiple uses may not be apparent; adjacent and outwardly similar residential buildings may have been subdivided into different numbers of sub-units, and the present use of a building can vary from its original purpose, e.g. a house used for offices or as a private hotel, or a mill as a warehouse, without advertising this fact to passers-by. Only an interview with the occupants can yield the required information in these circumstances. The method of survey in detailed studies of land use must often combine inspection with interviewing; neither method, by itself, will suffice for all purposes.

With this variety of uses existing together in certain localities, the current notations of approved town development plans and of the statutory land-use maps can be unrealistic. Areas are shown as primarily for residential, industrial, civic or residential use, *inter alia.* Implicit in these generalized land-use categories are the two assumptions that all components are equally suitable as companions and that other uses would be inappropriate. It might be, though, that residential and commercial admixtures were desirable in city centres, or industry employing married women and service-repair activities could be designed in conjunction with houses in a residential environment. Many redevelopment projects propose a mixture of appropriate uses, often with circulation and access at different levels. Where an intermixture of uses exists under current conditions this should be recorded and distinguished on large-scale land-use maps of the locality as a preliminary to the formulation of planning proposals. At smaller scales one solution would be to introduce an official notation for 'mixed uses'.[6]

Another possibility, though with rather different implications, has been put forward by an American authority.[7] His useful contribution, which introduces the element of historic change into the land-use map, is the concept of 'transition or conversion districts', with subcategories such as from residential to business or industrial, or from one form of residential to other forms (usually single-family houses to multi-family houses). Such areas of changing land-use characteristics, representative of the invasion and succession of uses in inner urban areas, can be recognized in many British cities. A classification of this type would be more meaningful than the attempt, inevitably artificial, to apportion a town into primary use zones. Such transition districts exist particularly on the fringe of central areas, in inner areas of towns containing a complex matrix of industry and housing, and along the frontages of main radial routes. Transition districts of social change, through the establishment of religious or racial groups, may also be defined at the smaller scales of presentation. It will often be revealing to compare the distribution of 'transition' districts with 'stable' areas, and to identify the different pressures and conditions which are involved.

Some reference has already been made to land ownership. This subject needs its own specialist study and assessment, but tends to intrude into land-use maps under various guises. Railway workers' cottages, their associated allotments, and dock areas have been shown on the official one-inch land-use maps as railway operational land; public playing fields in the grounds of a private institution will not be given a separate notation. The kind of land ownership may vitally influence the development of land and should therefore be studied. Extensive areas under a single ownership in or near town centres might facilitate redevelopment. It might prove extremely difficult for development agencies to acquire land owned by the British Transport Commission or the Ecclesiastical Commissioners, even if ripe for alternative development.

Many different methods of classification may be devised to suit the variety of circumstances in a planning area but, as with all planning studies, the land-use survey should be planned and programmed in advance to a standardized technique including the grouping and subgrouping of data, map scales and method of presentation. Land-use studies could avail themselves much more of existing classifications, such as the Census of Distribution for the different types of retail premises or the Classification of Industries for all buildings and land providing employment. These compilations are comprehensive, and could be adapted to suit local circumstances or the special requirements of a land-use investigation. The new land-use survey mentioned in Chapter 4 illustrates this approach, because manufacturing industry is recorded and subdivided on the basis of the industrial classification in the 1951 Census of Population. A rigid method for classifying and depicting land use has been devised by the planning Ministry to cover the existing and proposed uses of the land in England and Wales. A real danger exists that an uncritical acceptance and adherence to this classification and method of approach will conceal more information than it yields. The tendency is to record 'as per the book', rather than to think about the effects and the complications of each use. A new subject must experiment continually with its techniques, and seek always to improve upon its methods of recording and analysis.

The type and condition of buildings

Comprehensive surveys of the type and condition of buildings must generally be undertaken by field inspection, though certain external sources of information may be able to yield useful information about specific aspects or subjects. These include the fire brigade headquarters, antiquarian societies, local authority building inspectors and the factory inspectorate of the Ministry of Labour about industrial premises regarded as unsatisfactory through age, structural or other defects. The final assessment of quality and of useful life will demand from the field surveyor a considerable background knowledge of building construction and architectural form. Like most other planning surveys a specialist training is highly desirable.

Surveys should first be descriptive of existing conditions and character. A good example of this approach is provided by a recent study of housing types in Whitby.[8] The classification was first by age with the periods pre-1700, 1700–1840, 1840–75, 1875–1918, 1918–45 and post-1945 being regarded as significant. Against these periods of construction houses were then distinguished by their type, including large detached houses, country residences, small cottages, back-to-back houses, farmhouses, boarding houses in terraces, tunnel-back houses with and without front gardens, blocks of flats, and semi-detached and detached houses and bungalows. Elsewhere and for other purposes it might be appropriate to distinguish in modern housing between local authority, private dwellings, housing for special groups such as old persons, individual buildings with historic, aesthetic or symbolic significance, and property in various categories of obsolescence and in need of replacement. It should also be possible to locate distinctive vistas, to identify foci and axes and features with special development potentialities. The process of establishing the facts is almost without end and further considerations may be relevant such as the size of gardens, the amount, age, height and character of the tree-planting, the availability of garage and off-the-street parking space or the condition and character of streets.

Against this possible wealth of information the statutory requirements only stipulate that the condition of buildings be presented under four categories: war-damaged buildings, condemned buildings, buildings of architectural or historic interest, and other buildings.[9] The latter category is classified by age into before 1875, 1875–1914 and since 1914. Arising from this evidence and in conjunction with factors such as density, mixture of uses, lay-out and structural condition, three types of planning area are suggested for distinction. These are areas requiring early re-development, areas becoming obsolete but which still retain some years of useful life, and areas not likely to require redevelopment for many years. Detailed surveys of the condition of buildings would be most valuable in the first two types of area. They will help towards suggesting various priorities and the sequence of areas for improvement and/or redevelopment, quite apart from pro-viding an indication of the magnitude and type of problem to be resolved.

An excellent example of this detailed appraisal, and incidentally an excellent manual on the scientific method of survey procedure, has been prepared by the American Public Health Association.[10] Its stated purpose is to provide a standard system for the classifi-cation and objective assessment of the size and nature of the housing problem 'to delimit both slums and lesser problem areas, to distinguish between the nature of deficiencies in different places, and thus to indicate whether the solution lies in rehabilitation of present dwellings, in demolition and rehousing, or in ultimate conversion from residence to other uses . . . Factors covered for dwellings include the usual survey items such as toilet and bathing facilities and overcrowding. New indices have been developed for condition of repair, safety of egress, adequacy of heating and lighting, sanitary condition of the premises, and other items sig-nificant for health or safety. Criteria of overcrowding have been greatly sharpened as compared with the usual single index of persons per room. Descriptive characteristics such as family size, income, rent paid and type of structure are also reported, as a basis for classification and analysis of the deficiency findings. In presenting the dwellings results, distinction is made between relatively fixed physical conditions and the changeable factors of occupancy and maintenance, since remedial action must recognize the difference between these two types of defects.[11]

Each factor is then awarded a numerical score to provide a quantitative measurement of housing deficiencies. This scoring is undertaken subsequently in the office, as the function of the observer is to observe and to record facts. Each measure records deficiencies, and notes departures downwards from an acceptable standard. The higher scores thus indicate the worst conditions. The results for either houses or districts, rental classes or number of families per dwelling, or for any combination of categories, are immediately comparable.

The adaptation of these standards to British conditions, by discussion between the appropriate interests and sample surveys in a variety of localities, would represent a first stage in assessing the size of the housing problem. Such studies are not prohibitive in cost; a study of 15,000 dwelling units at New Haven in 1944 cost $4,000 for the hire of personnel and covered enumeration, scoring and standard analysis of dwelling data, and costs would be reduced considerably per unit if the survey was more comprehensive and if existing staff were used for the collection of data. Sampling might also be used, as a survey of a small proportion of houses would indicate those areas for a complete coverage.

The cost is negligible compared with the cost of a redevelopment programme. A full appreciation of the facts removes prejudice from assessing either the size of the problem or the sequence of priorities based on the physical quality of dwellings. It can be demonstrated that in many areas where conditions are poor, clearance will be slow because of the sheer magnitude of the problem, hence planning programmes should be introduced to offset further deterioration and to extend the useful life of the buildings. The authentic facts from surveys of this character might also generate an enthusiasm for tackling the problems of slums and the blighted areas, and for arresting the process of decay elsewhere.

The assessment of the condition of industrial buildings raises many problems. Access and observation may not be so easy as with housing, greater variations exist in the structure of buildings, large units have a variety of different buildings within their boundary, and many premises serve specialized functions demanding techno-logical knowledge for their evaluation. The West Midland Group devised a pointing system based on factors such as siting, structure, lighting and sanitation, but this proved unduly elaborate and reliance was ultimately placed on a visual survey by one investigator to ensure a constant standard.[12] Three broad categories were distinguished. Buildings were classified as 'bad' when suffering from age or bad structural conditions to such an extent as to justify their immediate replacement under a replanning scheme; included int his class were houses converted into workshops and offices, old narrow workshops erected in the nineteenth century with low ceilings, timber floors and inadequate natural lighting. Buildings appearing to be reasonably satisfactory premises in fair-to-good structural condition were classified as in 'moderate' condition; they possessed one or more of the characteristics of 'bad' buildings that their replacement will be required within the next 30 years. 'Good' buildings were structurally sound, and included most of the factories built since 1914.

Further relevant factors would be the different types of premises occupied by the various industrial groups, their demands for storage space and access requirements, the extent to which the site was developed or otherwise used, and the opportunities for further development within the present site boundaries. An interesting study in this field has examined the characteristics of buildings with total floor areas of more than 7,500 square feet in Philadelphia.[13] The survey covered the assessed value of land and building area; external considerations such as land coverage, parking and loading facilities, and access; the age, type of construction and condition of the building; the ceiling height, floor-loading capacity, column spacing and condition of the ground and upper floors; the lay-out within a building and between associated buildings; the size, capacity and accessibility of elevators; and services including water, gas, electricity and heating. Each factor was allocated a value according to its relative importance and its condition; for example, off-street loading was deemed more important than air conditioning and could be rated from one to nine (air conditioning one to four). Composite graphs were prepared for each building, showing each factor and its level of rating, to provide a means either of comparing the condition of different buildings, or of comparing a selected building with a good building, or the average of buildings in one area with the average elsewhere.

Planning surveys of many other building subjects might also

be appropriate, e.g. office or hotel accommodation in central areas, or shops of varying type, size, function and location. Special studies of particular buildings may also be necessary as when the processes of economic or social change leave in their wake obsolete or vacant premises. To what extent may these buildings be adapted for some alternative use? The Cotton Reorganization Scheme, for example, was concerned with the scrapping of machinery, but not with the re-use for some other activity of the empty mills. A planning survey in such localities would elucidate the characteristics of these buildings and their sites, and examine their possibilities for alternative industrial or other purposes. Space, load capacity, access, fire risks, availability of services, storage facilities, structural condition, probable rents, possibilities of subdivision or subletting and other elements would each receive their own careful examination. Surveys of individual buildings would also be relevant when considering the amount of property acquisition involved in the siting of alternative routes for road improvement proposals. Housing areas becoming obsolescent, but retaining several years of useful life, merit detailed study so that the necessary short-term improvements to the environment and building can be effected. The problem of large family houses, outmoded through the decreasing number of large families and the social changes with regard to servants, deserves more attention than it has received over recent years.

Density surveys

'Density, in relation to planning, means . . . the number of objects—houses, rooms, persons, etc.—per unit of space. Detailed information about density is of vital importance for planning purposes, for upon it are based most of the proposals for reducing congestion. The subject is a difficult one and no completely adequate technique has yet emerged.'[14] Densities provide an important means of influencing standards. The present discussion will be concerned with their measurement and calculation, rather than with their use in particular planning circumstances.

Residential densities may be overall, gross or net and much confusion has arisen from a failure to appreciate the distinction between these terms. Like can only be compared with like; gross densities can never be compared with net densities, or gross densities with gross densities if the physical basis is different. Net area refers to small residential groups containing the same type of house, and includes the sites of houses and their curtilage, incidental areas of small private and public open space, and half the width of any adjoining street up to a maximum of 20 feet. A gross density describes the characteristics of a predominantly residential district and, in addition to the net area, includes primary schools, local shops and offices, public houses, open space, local service industries and half the width of any street up to a maximum of 20 feet; secondary schools are not included. Overall densities can refer either to the total area under predominantly urban uses, to the total area of land in a town map area, or to the total area of land in a local authority boundary.

Residential densities can be expressed in different ways, and each has merits and limitations. The practice pre-war was to use the concept of 'houses per acre', which had the advantages of being readily understood and easily calculated but which did not indicate variations between the size of houses. Three separate densities are now used: the number of habitable rooms per acre or 'accommodation density', the number of persons resident per acre or 'population density', and the number of persons resident per habitable room or the 'occupancy rate'.

Information on the number of habitable rooms can be obtained through the local authority building inspectors, from the housing department for local authority housing, from the records of the planning authority for post-1948 housing or from the regional offices of the electricity boards. The difficulties involved in classification have already been discussed. In similar adjacent houses one kitchen can be used for meals and living purposes, and in the other for cooking and washing-up only; likewise one house can have a through-lounge and its neighbour a dining-room and a living-room; are the box-rooms in the two houses both used as bedrooms?

The principal disadvantages of 'accommodation density' as a means towards understanding the situation are that the size of rooms remains undisclosed; the term itself and its calculation, the division of the number of habitable rooms by the net area of land in acres, is confusing to lay planning committees; the expression 60 rooms per acre means less to the general public than does 12 houses per acre. It offers no advantage over the earlier concept of housing units per acre which, together with the average square feet of living space per house unit, would suffice together with population density. There would then be information on the number of units per acre, the size of these units, and the number of people living in them. In any case, accommodation density should be calculated only for predominantly residential areas; it becomes meaningless when applied to houses above shops, flats in central areas, or residential accommodation in institutions. The Ministry of Town and Country Planning (Circular 63) suggests that in houses occupied by a single family rooms over six should be ignored, but this approach assumes that information about family distribution is available separately for every house, and results in an apparent increase in accommodation density when such units are converted into flats. Four- and five-bedroomed houses are also required by the larger family groups. Neither accuracy nor completeness can ever result from ignoring an element.

Residential density may also be stated in terms of 'population density'. This should be calculated for the same areas as above. The problem is how to estimate the number of people. The only statistical source is the electoral register, and the exclusion of children and other non-voting groups has already been discussed in Chapter 2. Any weighting-up to a total population in every residential block assumes an even distribution of children over the ward or parish. If the education authority has conducted a recent survey into the number of children in each house, information from this source can be used. If not, the only alternative is a stratified random survey of different house types and areas, but this is time-consuming and best combined with a more comprehensive survey on a further range of subjects.

'Occupancy rate' is the third density of current practice. It is calculated by dividing either the number of persons within an area by the number of rooms, or the population density by the accommodation density. The result purports to show the volume of overcrowding, but the important factors of size of rooms, sex, age, household relationships and family attitudes are excluded and the concept of 'residential floor area per person' might be more meaningful. Occupancy rate has a usefulness in general rather than in specific terms, but suffers from the cumulative disadvantages discussed above in both its numerator and denominator.

For non-residential areas official reliance is placed on the 'floor-space index', which is the total floor space of the building divided by the area of the site to depict the intensity of use for each site or street block.[15] The floor space of a building is taken to be the sum of the roofed area of the building at each floor level including all wall thicknesses, internal circulation space and ancillary accommodation. The site area includes half the width of the adjacent streets. As the concern is with the relationship between the buildings and the site the inclusion of the adjoining roads is a needless complication, and the 'plot ratio' of the London County Council provides a more convenient index to suggest the intensity of use and of concentration in certain localities.[16] This ratio is the same as the floor-space index, except that the street widths are excluded. A plot ratio of two means either that a two-storey building covers the whole of the site or a four-storey building covers half the site, and so on, according to the form of the building.

In industrial areas various densities may be devised, though each can be misleading in certain circumstances. The site coverage by industrial buildings can be indicated by a proportion and the density of multi-storey industrial buildings such as cotton mills by a plot ratio, but the vacant land may be used for access, storage or unloading. Also a plot ratio for office buildings enjoys a fairly constant application to the height of floors, a factor which is not present in industrial processes such as oil refineries, gas works, power stations or assembly shops. Concepts such as operatives per acre, per site or per 1,000 square feet of ground area or floor space may be estimated. Difficulties of calculation include seasonal fluctuations in employment, the operation of shift systems, differences in occupational status and whether employees work at or away from the premises.

Density measurements provide essential tools of planning

analysis, but also appear on development plans and policy statements as planning objectives. The plot ratio in zone 'x' of the central
area shall not exceed 3·5; 150 acres of land at 'y' are zoned for
residential development at 90 rooms per acre. The requirements
must therefore be capable of interpretation in clear and unambiguous terms by the public in general and by developers in
particular, quite apart from their technical use and handling by
the planning profession. It is doubtful whether the present measures
satisfy these criteria. There is considerable scope for refinements
and clarification in the method of approach, especially with
residential densities and particularly with the concept of a room.

Environmental influences and possibilities

Density considerations have extended the planning appreciation of
the land use and building patterns outwards from the individual
unit to measure its degree of concentration in the surrounding
environment. Sensory surveys of the sources, distribution and
volume of noise, the localized incidence of dust and grit, air pollution and the visual qualities of the area are important. Environmental factors examined in the previous assessment of housing
conditions by the American Public Health Association included
'crowding of the land by buildings, intermixture of business and
industrial uses with residences, proximity to major traffic routes
and railroads, adequacy of public utilities, and availability of
essential community services: schools, transportation, parks and
playgrounds'.[17] The character of a neighbourhood is assessed for
example on factors which include the number of dangerous road
crossings between home and school, the width and condition of
pavements, the setback of the house from traffic routes, the distance
to the nearest playfield and the proximity to noise, smoke, smell
and glare at nights.

The intrusion of alien or nonconforming uses, or the presence
of vacant premises, which affect the character of an established area,
provide early indications of potential change and a warning signal
that planned action might be appropriate. Such studies of blight
and of probable blight, when coupled with surveys of the potential

of vacant land, yield information about the two basic processes of urban growth and change—renewal in blighted areas, and expansion in areas of land potential. 'The fact is, however, that little has been done on the technical level to identify and define the elements that constitute . . . blight, to develop systematic means for observing and describing such blight, or to supply objective measures of its seriousness.'[18]

The study of vacant land may be confined to unused land within the urban limits and to open land at the fringe of the urban area. The concern of the survey is to determine the suitability of these sites for development, and their potential for different categories of use such as residential, industrial and public open space. The considerations involved are many and include the physical factors discussed previously, points of existing and possible access for road (principally) and rail (possibly), legal or other public or private restrictions on use, and the position with regard to public services (see below).

The total quantity of vacant land will have emerged from the land-use survey; an appreciation of the land's potential and its deficiencies requires a separate appraisal. Many forms of classification may be designed. Categories might distinguish between the size of areas available, slope (the requirement of large single-storey factories will be for flat land), degrees of availability (e.g. immediately available with all public services or available in five years' time when a main drainage scheme is complete), improvements which are required (lacking access but other facilities all available), and the characteristics of adjoining uses which will limit the use of each vacant site to a restricted range of development activities.

Presentation of this data must permit cross-reference between the various factors, as different forms of development will not have the same requirements and needs. Also, not all factors will prove of equal significance for every potential user. One site may be suitable for industry or housing, another only industry, and another for industry or public open space. Perhaps the most appropriate method will be a series of overlays each depicting a separate factor; alternatively, though this tends to be confusing because of the amount of detail, all information can be presented on one composite map.

In either instance summary statistics of vacant land under various classifications and potential uses should be tabulated.

Public utilities require their own separate surveys, as a factor which influences the potentialities of vacant or unused land. Electricity, water and gas supply, sewage disposal and special facilities for the disposal or treatment of obnoxious material should be studied. The information to be gleaned will include the statutory areas of supply, the routes and capacities of mains and grids, whether or not services are used to their full potential, the location and site expansion requirements of all fixed plant, the areas served from the existing systems, areas which could be served from the existing system (a factor which will have to be estimated in conjunction with physical conditions such as slope) and areas which will be capable of being served when new development proposals have been completed. These categories of detail will be valuable in showing possible locations for planned development such as town and village extensions, industrial sites and housing estates and also in making full use of existing utilities.

Conclusion

Planning is a discipline in which the understanding of spatial relationships is essential. Detailed land-use surveys are fundamental to the whole process of planning thought and positive action. The planning ministry have suggested notations for official use by Local Planning Authorities in the preparation of land-use maps and in the recording of anticipated land uses on development plans, but their scope requires to be improved considerably for a fuller understanding and appreciation of present complexities and problems. Land use should be regarded as a dynamic response to social and economic conditions. Areas of transition, of conversion, of existing and of probable blight, of clearance and redevelopment, or suitable for potential development in a variety of categories should be recognized and grades of policy formulated on the basis of ascertainable facts. Land-use surveys and building studies, the appreciation of density of concentration, and the assessment of environmental condition and quality are interlocking surveys. Their

128 SURVEYS FOR TOWN AND COUNTRY PLANNING

purpose is to advance planning thought, to enlighten the public, and to show the possibilities inherent within the present position. These survey subjects are complex. They should not be separated in their overall implications for land-use development from either the previous 'physical' surveys or the content of subsequent chapters. No one planning survey transcends in importance the synoptic vision of all factors operating in a given area and together indicating the future potential.

1 Ministry of Town and Country Planning, Circular no. 40, *Survey for Development Plans*, H.M.S.O., 1948.

2 P. Geddes, *Cities in Evolution*, 1949, p. xxx.

3 Ministry of Housing and Local Government, Circular no. 9/55, *First Review of Approved Development Plans*, H.M.S.O., 1955.

4 M. Smith, 'A Lands Record System for a County Planning Department,' *Journal of the Town Planning Institute*, vol. XLV, 1959, pp. 236–8. A. Morris, 'Land Use Analysis by Punched Cards', *Journal of the Town Planning Institute*, vol. XLV, 1959, pp.163–7.

5 Ministry of Town and Country Planning, Circulars no. 63, *Report of the Survey*, H.M.S.O., 1949, and no. 92, *Reproduction of Survey and Development Plan Maps*, H.M.S.O., 1951

6 L. Keeble, *Principles and Practice of Town and Country Planning*, Estates Gazette, 1959, p. 97 and appendix I.

7 C. Woodbury (ed.), *The Future of Cities and Urban Redevelopment*, 1955.

8 M. R. G. Conzen in G. H. J. Daysh (ed.) *A Survey of Whitby and the Surrounding Area*, 1958, pp. 50–77.

9 Circulars no. 40 and 63, op. cit.

10 American Public Health Association, *An Appraisal Method for Measuring the Quality of Housing*, part I, 'Nature and Uses of the Method', 1945; part II (3 vols.), 'Appraisal of Dwelling Conditions', 1946; part III, 'Appraisal of Neighbourhood Environment', 1950.

11 Ibid, part I, pp. 6–8.

12 West Midland Group, *Conurbation*, 1948, ch. IX.

13 A. D. Little, *The Usefulness of Philadelphia's Industrial Plant*, Report to the Philadelphia City Planning Commission, January 1960.

14 Keeble, op. cit., p. 97. The application of densities is examined in many Ministry handbooks and housing manuals.

15 Ministry of Town and Country Planning, *Advisory Handbook on the Redevelopment of Central Areas*, H.M.S.O., 1947.

16 L.C.C., *A Plan to Combat Congestion in Central London*, 1957.

17 American Public Health Association, op. cit., part I, p. 8.

18 C. Woodbury (ed.), *Urban Redevelopment: Problems and Practices*, 1953, p. 41.

6

COMMUNICATION, TRAFFIC AND PARKING SURVEYS

LAND use and transportation have many broad areas of overlap and for many reasons are closely interwoven. Specialized types of land use exist within the city, and this differentiation by function could not have emerged without modern transport arrangements. Cities in their present form would be impossible without facilities for the extensive movement of people and of goods. It is transport which permits the concentration of a labour force and manufacturing materials at specific points, which allows people to live away from their place of work, or which permits the development of a locality. The radius of an urban sphere of influence, and hence of a town's size and character, reflects the nodality and extent of its transport connections and facilities. The quantity of land under streets, highways, railways, canals, airfields, docks and parking space may exceed a quarter of the developed area, or be greater than any other land-use element. Planning for land use and traffic movement cannot be regarded as separate exercises, but are complementary to each other. Traffic provides a means whereby the goals of city and regional planning might be achieved.

Many complex problems exist within this extensive field. Perhaps the most fundamental is a full appreciation of the fact that, with all its attendant advantages and disadvantages, the motor vehicle has come to stay. The impact yet to be experienced is that traffic volumes will double, treble and quadruple within the life span of our younger generations. An ostrich-like or restrictive approach to this inevitable situation will not suffice.

As the inherited road system and the physical form of developed areas are inadequate to meet the exacting demands of modern transport, a considerable body of accurate knowledge and factual information is required before proposals can be recommended and implemented. The valuable work of the Road Research Laboratory is concerned primarily with the engineering and technical considerations of road design and traffic safety,[1] and a new profession of traffic engineering is emerging, combining the scientific methods of investigation with the technical acumen of the engineer. In the words of one proponent, 'it is necessary to find out what traffic there is, where it wants to go and its purpose . . . This is the primary task of the traffic engineer'.[2] This knowledge also provides a very definite field of study for the planner. Traffic is generated by the pattern of land use, its movement is influenced by the spacing of settlements, and traffic volumes on particular routes are affected by the location and siting of new developments. Roads, like railways, have traffic and development functions, and the complex series of relationships must be appreciated by the land-use planner. In the evocative phrase of Mitchell and Rapkin, traffic is a function of land use.[3]

The network of communications and accessibility

An initial range of information should be obtained on the routes, quality and function of all components in the network of communications. For roads the requisite minimum information is the existing road pattern and the Ministry of Transport classification. The position of obstacles such as steep hills with their gradients, low bridges with their height, bottlenecks with their width and weak bridges with their weight limitations should be presented diagrammatically. The position of accidents may be plotted from police records and will provide an instructive exercise in that certain black spots requiring road improvement will emerge from a study of the map; elsewhere relationship between accidents and shopping streets which function as loading bays for shops, a moving belt for traffic, a space for parked vehicles, a crossing point for pedestrians and a social meeting place for shoppers will bear silent witness to the fact that urban planning in the form of pedestrian precincts and traffic segregation can reduce accidents more than road improvements conceived in isolation. Stretches of road with dual carriageway or which have otherwise been improved, realigned or regraded, and places where improvements are required through either the volume of congestion or other factors should be shown. The position of car parks, lay-bys and off-the-street parking facilities, together with their capacity, should also be noted as an integral part of the road network. It may be desirable to extend this factual survey, and to record the position of buildings which serve road traffic such as garages, transport cafés and bus depots.

Other means of transportation will also require study. Railways should be classified by their number of tracks, and whether or not subject to modernization. The position of stations needs to be recorded, distinguishing between those providing goods and passenger services and those with goods or passenger services only. With passenger stations a further distinction exists between passenger stations served by local trains only, and those with express services.[4] For usable canals and navigable rivers the range of survey information might comprise the routes together with the details of maximum permissible beam and draught for boats, the position of obstacles such as locks or where speed limitations operate through insecure banks or long tunnels, the position of wharves and whether modernized, and stretches which enjoy uses such as pleasure boating, fishing, a particular amenity significance or in frequent use as footpaths. With airfields the only relevant information for broader planning purposes is the direction of the main runways, and the areas along approach routes with zoning restrictions on the height of buildings.

The function of the different transport routes must be appreciated. Certain railway routes offer main-line services between the principal towns or regions of the country, other lines transport suburban dwellers to and from the regional capital twice daily. With roads an important functional distinction exists between arterial, inter-urban, cross-town, feeder, local and service roads and these differences should be reflected in the associated land-use arrangements, design capacities, the type and frequency of junctions, and so on; this grading of roads by function cannot be equated with the Ministry of Transport system of road classification and numbering.

Physical information about the routes, functions and facilities of the transportation network will provide the basis for an assessment of its utilization and of its activities in serving other land uses. The concern will be with the genesis, destination, volume, direction and trends of traffic flow in all the various categories. A discussion of the data required for roads will follow. Other transport services are different in that much information is available in the records of the authorities concerned, though access to this raw material varies and its interpretation may require a considerable understanding of transport economics. Introductory material should include, for railways, the number of fast and slow stopping trains per day at each station, the frequency of trains to nearby centres throughout the day and at peak travel periods, the volume of passenger and of goods traffic handled, the trends, and the direction, of regular passenger travel; for canals, wharves and depots, traffic volumes, capacities and trends together with details of any emphasis on particular types of goods; for docks and airfields, passenger and goods statistics as above. In addition studies of the inward and outward movement of goods may prove of particular planning significance because their processing, treatment or use in manufacture will often provide the basis for industrial activity (including specialized offices, markets and warehousing) and influence strongly the allocation of land for specific purposes in the port or airfield precincts.

The survey details about the transport network and its services are brought together in an appreciation of accessibility. There is first the physical accessibility to routes, and useful maps can be prepared to show places within half a mile of frequent daily and infrequent market-day bus services, and also of railway stations. The map details must recognize barriers to communication such as steep slopes and rivers, canals or railways without bridging points, rather than be generalized at standard distances 'as the crow flies' from each transport service. In remote and rural areas access to public telephones is important, and areas not within specific distances of this public service should be portrayed diagrammatically.

The details of physical accessibility by distance should be supplemented by the quality of accessibility in time. Two separate elements are involved—areas situated within certain travelling times from the centre under study, and areas accessible by public transport at certain significant times of the day. The first factor, time-distance, may be plotted direct from time-tables. The usual method is to note the time along each route by the fastest service, allowing 10 minutes for the journey from office and shops to bus or railway station for the accessibility of central areas, and assuming a walking speed of 3 m.p.h. from the unloading points. The resultant isochrones, or lines of equal time distance, will appear as circles round railway stations and as narrowing bands along bus routes; they provide a valuable indication of relative accessibility to various districts. With regard to the incidence of rural depopulation, for example, does any correlation exist between trends in inter-urban areas well served by bus services and population trends in areas with poorer services? Another pertinent analysis may be to examine whether a significant relationship exists between population trends and areas accessible to a range of employment opportunities before 8 a.m. in the morning? Which areas are accessible from evening entertainment centres after 9 p.m., 10 p.m. and 11 p.m.? The siting of factories in rural areas can be influenced substantially by the nodality of a situation within the catchment area of a potential labour supply.

The importance of inter-accessibility between different transport facilities must also be understood, for both passenger and freight requirements. The problem has its specialized aspects such as the planning of terminals, the interconnection and traffic flow between food markets and railway goods terminals or port facilities, and the transfer of passengers with the minimum of congestion from air to road or from long-distance rail to local bus services. With goods traffic there must be sorting facilities for the breakdown of large consignments and for the assembly of small loads for their destination, quite apart from the physical connection between the different modes of transport. These developments are fixed in location and yet exert a great impact on land-use patterns, traffic movement and land values. Plans for modernization and changes should be conceived in broader terms than the facility itself; they must take into account the interchange and interflow which exist, for example, between roads and railways, railways and industrial areas, rapid transit routes and high-quality residential areas. A planning policy which emerges from the study of one factor in a total environment of many relationships will be biased. Awareness of the mutual impact and repercussions can emerge only when surveys are designed to elucidate the interplay between several elements in a given situation.

Vehicle parking surveys[3]

Parking provides a special example of a terminal facility, in that it involves the transfer from a motor vehicle to a pedestrian movement. The driver becomes a pedestrian, but the requirements of both must be met in the provision of parking facilities. A preliminary survey of the parked vehicle will be of parking concentration, to yield information upon the number of parked vehicles at the kerbside and in off-the-street parking localities. These facts may be noted by an observer travelling through the area on foot or as a car passenger, and the number of vehicles observed may be plotted directly on to large-scale base maps. The data are of areas in use, and from the statistics may be calculated the proportion of vehicles in different types of location such as car parks, side-roads, rear-access roads and main roads. If the survey of parking concentration is undertaken at different times of the day then comparisons of the differential use of areas throughout the day can be made. A further extension of the survey would yield information about areas of pressure on different days of the week. Meat markets, fruit and vegetable markets, magistrates' courts and shops have considerable daily fluctuations in the demand for parking space. If surveys are undertaken over more extensive periods of time, then trends in the numbers of parked vehicles may perhaps be estimated.

Of greater value than the simple number of parked vehicles at any one time are *duration* surveys or the observation of the length of time for which vehicles are parked. The simplest method is for an observer to note the registration numbers and letters of vehicles at regular intervals, perhaps every 15 minutes or half-hourly should the

136 SURVEYS FOR TOWN AND COUNTRY PLANNING

concern not be primarily with the short-term parker. The observer will work round his circuit in the same direction at each separate count; the time spent in covering the circuit must be less than the interval between observations. Tabulations can be prepared to show the length of time for which vehicles are parked, the variations which exist in this length of time for different classes of vehicle or in different locations; and information is also yielded on the total number of parked vehicles as above. The length of parking attains a particular importance because the long-term parker provides the greatest problem as far as the occupation of space is concerned, whereas short-term parkers may be the greatest proportion of the vehicles parking but only a small proportion of those parked at any one time.

The planner now knows where the vehicles are parked and for what length of time. The next stage of the investigation will be to understand the need for the distribution of parking spaces in different parts of the city. Apart from asking parkers the impracticable question, 'How far would you be willing to walk from this car?', three methods of survey may be suggested. The first is to ask people when returning to their parked vehicle about places visited and, for all-day parkers, the location of their place of work and whether the vehicle is required during working hours. Alternatively, random samples of office workers, shop customers and people in the streets of the town centre could be asked questions about their method of travel to the centre and, if by car, where it is parked and for how long. One further possibility would be to place questionnaires in the form of stamped and addressed postcards under the windscreen wipers of parked cars; questions could be asked about the length of parking, the purpose of the journey, frequency of parking, places visited whilst the car was parked and attitude to parking fees; the principal advantage of this method is that it overcomes the difficulties of interviewing the owners of vehicles parked in a variety of different places and arriving and departing at sundry times, but the proportion of non-response will be higher.

What need for parking space is generated by a building? Four different categories of information would be required. One, the vehicles used by persons employed in the building, which represents a need for long-term parking space from persons employed in the building and a demand for space which need not be in the vicinity of the building. Two, the vehicles used by customers, visitors, clients and travellers. The demand from these groups will vary throughout the day and will tend in most instances to be a short-term need; many callers will be able to travel a limited distance from their vehicle, and several will be making visits to other buildings. Other callers, especially travellers with samples, will require nearby or internal parking accommodation. Three, service vehicles which are likewise mainly short-term callers and are of many different categories including G.P.O. vans, milk deliveries, coal, oil, stationery and canteen supplies; these vehicles should not park at the kerbside in busy city streets. Four, the vehicles which operate from the building including delivery and collection vans, and cars used for business purposes by members of the staff. The total demands for parking space generated by these categories, and the variations between different types of use remains very much of an unknown quantity.

One function of such surveys will be to assess parking standards, which are fundamental for development control decisions in connection with new development, and for the allocation of space in redevelopment projects. Standards should be calculated separately for each type of use, such as one space per 'x' office workers, 'y' spaces per 100 hospital beds and 'z' spaces per so many hotel bedrooms. In residential localities the standards for the provision of garage space might vary as between private and local authority housing, to the situation of districts relative to the major centres of employment, and to differences in the size and income bracket of families. The research worker is concerned with assessing the demand for parking space; the alternative methods of incorporating these requirements within the design will be examined at a later stage in the planning process.

Traffic surveys

A simple volumetric count of the number of vehicles passing along a road has many implications, for example upon the design of road junctions, improvement schemes, priorities for road construction, traffic control and the strength of foundations. The total flow over a period of time may be recorded, distinguishing between the different types of vehicles and the volume of movement at different times of the day (preferably at 10- or 15-minute intervals). It is however usually important to know, as additional information to the quantity of traffic and its direction of movement, the traffic's place of origin, its destination and its intermediate calls. Information might be required on the amount and direction of through traffic, for the construction of bypasses or relief roads for vehicles passing through towns, and also on the origin, routes and first points of call for traffic generated in the town. With this knowledge it is possible to distinguish between three different types of traffic with their differing needs—through traffic with both terminals outside a city, regional traffic with one terminal outside the city, and internal traffic with both terminals within the city.

The first technique of investigation is by direct interview, when either all or a random sample of vehicles are halted. The driver is asked certain predetermined questions, which must be few in number, simply phrased, short and to the point in order to reduce congestion to a minimum. This method provides the most complete and accurate results with the minimum of bias and can, if required, provide full details of the whole journey with routes taken by each vehicle; this completeness is impossible by the other methods of traffic survey.

The principal criticisms are that traffic control is necessary, as only a uniformed police officer has the legal right to halt moving traffic and some delays to certain vehicles are inevitable. This may be reduced to the minimum by good advertising at the census points, the efficient handling of traffic, clear advance signs to indicate the questions, and cards in bold letters to show the questions asked.[6] Traffic congestion may also be minimized by the use of sampling techniques, though this method is not yet employed extensively in British traffic surveys.

The general underlying principles of a sample survey will have emerged from the discussion in Chapter 3. Each vehicle must have an equal chance of selection to avoid bias. One method would be to stratify the flow of traffic by the type of vehicles involved. The size of the sample for interview would depend on the volume of vehicles in each category at the different times of day and on the proportion of vehicles which could be interviewed. A random selection of every 'n'th vehicle in each category would be directed from the main traffic flow into the interviewing bay—say every 10th lorry, every 5th cyclist, every 25th private vehicle, though these proportions could be varied in a predetermined manner to accord with the conditions of traffic flow. Alternatively sampling could be on a time basis with say every 'n'th vehicle halted in the first half-minute of every three- or five-minute period. The use of sampling to reduce traffic congestion and to provide comparable information to a full survey still requires an efficient organization at each census point, but only a percentage of traffic need be delayed and this for a short period by efficient traffic control.

The advantages of the direct-interview method over other possible methods of approach are that *all* the required data are acquired at each census point. The facts do not require to be 'matched' with material from elsewhere, and vehicles need be stopped only once. A complete ring of points round a given area is not necessary. In a survey of traffic generation and of through traffic around a town, the check points on each main radial road need interview only outgoing traffic. The questions 'Where did your journey begin?' and, for traffic which did not originate locally, 'Did you make a call in the town?' and 'What was your route of entry into the town?' will yield information on total traffic flow, the proportions of through traffic and the routes of entry into and departure from the town—in each case by type of vehicles and by time of day as required. It is preferable to interview outgoing rather than ingoing traffic; the question 'Have you stopped in the town?' elicits a more reliable response than 'Do you intend to stop in the town?'; also, of course, a survey of inward traffic does not assess the volume of traffic generated within the town. The final, and very substantial, advantage of interviewing drivers is the high response rate. This should be almost 100 per cent as the purpose of traffic surveys is, quite simply, to benefit the road user. Direct inter-viewing with sampling of one in every three vehicles was used, for example, in the recent prediction of the possible volumes of traffic expected to use the Tyne vehicular tunnel.[7]

A second method is by the observation of registration numbers, which involves a complete cordon of the area covering every point of entry and departure. The registration numbers of all vehicles entering and leaving, together with the times of arrival and departure, are noted. These number have to be 'matched' at the analysis stage and, if the journey exceeds a certain time, then a call is presumed. The principal advantages are that drivers are not stopped, though vehicles may be slowed down to permit registration numbers to be recorded, and drivers need not even be aware that a census is being undertaken. These somewhat marginal advantages are more than offset by the many disadvantages of this method. These include the possibilities of an error when recording numbers and the laborious task of matching literally thousands of numbers: the count must be continuous over a period of time to permit 'matching' whereas interviews can be limited to certain significant times of the day, and a survey of registration numbers is not practicable in hours of darkness. Sampling may, however, be used to reduce the volume of work. It is not possible to record vehicle registrations beginning with certain predetermined letters because these are associated with the locality of initial registration and would thus introduce a bias in selection, but sampling of the registration *numbers* could be used as these enjoy no special sequence; for example, only numbers beginning with say 3, 7 and 8 need be recorded—the actual selection of numbers would be by random means.

These disadvantages do not offset the slight inconvenience to a proportion of drivers by interviewing but may be diminished by the use either of postcards or of coloured tags. In the postcard method vehicles are stopped, are handed pre-paid postcards, which should be completed and returned to the survey organization. The operative word is 'should'; only a proportion of the cards are returned and this response is not necessarily representative. The supposed advantages over interviewing are that the driver's time is not wasted and fewer staff are required than for full interviewing, but random sampling provides the same advantages. The method of postcards, though still widely employed, is not to be recommended because of the bias through non-response; the method can be expected to become outmoded when the possibilities of random sampling become more widely appreciated. It will retain some limited value for *ad hoc* inquiries where there is a stream of slow moving or halted traffic—in a traffic jam, at dock gates, at level crossings or waiting for a ferry. But even so, why pass over a postcard which may not be returned when a few well-chosen questions to every 'n'th vehicle would provide the same information immediately?

The fourth method is to place coloured tags on vehicles. The vehicle is stopped and a label, using a different colour for each point of entry, is affixed. Some drivers may object to being branded, and others may dislike adhesives on their polished vehicle. On the other hand the method is valuable when it is necessary to plot the course taken by vehicles through a complex locality with many alternative routes, for example, in a central area. A corps of observers stationed about the area can plot the passage of vehicles by their coloured tags, and their progress throughout the town can be analysed subsequently. The method is more reliable and simpler than the observation of registration numbers, but vehicles have to be stopped once.

The fifth possible method does not involve the traffic itself, but would discover information about travel, journeys made, routes followed, dates and times of journeys, interchange between different forms of communication, numbers of passengers, types of goods carried, and so on through interviews and questionnaires. The coverage could be of industries and of commercial establishments, by car owners, and/or by place of residence or workplace. The survey by the Ministry of Transport into the mileage and tonnage carried by goods vehicles has been mentioned previously. The same author has examined a sample survey of expenditure by 13,000 households, undertaken in 1953–4 by the Ministry of Labour, to show the expenditure on transport and vehicles by households living in urban and rural areas and to determine the amount of travel generated in different types of area.[8] The *London Travel Surveys* of 1949 and 1954 provide further examples of this type of investigation.[9]

Surveys of traffic generated by buildings have been discussed previously relative to the assessment of needs for parking space. From the same sources can be established the details of traffic movement to and from buildings, and ultimately of the traffic generated by different land-use zones, its direction and volume of movement, and any special transport or movement relationships which exist between different land-use zones within the city. These considerations will have an obvious bearing on factors such as density, the possibilities of dispersal, and the siting of new and related developments. Such studies are as yet in their infancy; they represent a fruitful field for teamwork between traffic engineers and land-use planners. The principal need is for the surveys to be undertaken under competent direction, and then for the results to be applied in planning and highway decisions.

In these latter types of travel and traffic surveys the collection of information is spread out over a greater period of time than in the more typical count or origin and destination surveys of moving traffic, but the results yield more complete information on attitudes, types of journey, daily and weekly fluctuations, and on the relationships between traffic and land use. Their organization, even for a relatively small area of town, demands a considerable staff over a period of time. They are not surveys to be embarked upon lightly without adequate preparation and assessment of the costs involved. The results should however lead to a far greater understanding of travel habits and movement than is yet known for most British areas.

As far as presentation is concerned, it is important to distinguish between travel lines, the actual magnitude of movement in the streets surveyed, and desire lines, or the straight line which connects the points of origin and destination. In either diagram the pattern is usually depicted by varying the width of the lines. Data may be presented for all traffic or to distinguish between the various categories of vehicle, and by time for the whole census period, peak hours or otherwise as significant. The diagrams will be essential to clarify the mass of statistical data, and to show in relation to the distribution of land uses the patterns of actual and desired movements.

Pedestrian surveys require separate mention, as techniques for measurement are somewhat different from traffic surveys. Volumetric counts as previously will yield the number of persons passing a given point. If all points of entry and exit to a street or building are covered then in theory continuous counts of entrants and departures, together with the number within the survey area at the start of the count, will give the numbers present at any subsequent time. In practice cumulative errors will invalidate the results. The solution is the principle of the moving observer. 'To obtain an estimate of the number of people in a street, the observer traverses the street in one direction, counting all the people he passes, in whichever direction they are moving, and deducting all the people who overtake him. He then re-traverses the street in the opposite direction, moving at the same speed and counting as before. If this is done the average of the two counts gives an estimate of the average number of people in the street during the time of the counts. If people are mostly moving in one direction the count in this direction will be reduced, but the count in the opposite direction will be correspondingly increased.'[10] This method may be used to estimate the number of people in streets, precincts, shops and elsewhere at different times of the day. Streets and large shop floors can, of course, be subdivided into smaller areas for survey by different observers.

The observation or interviewing of pedestrians may be desirable. Observation could record the movement of people in a traffic-free shopping precinct or their behaviour at a road junction in different traffic circumstances; interviews could reveal the mode of travel into the survey area, and such items as the distance of movement from a parked car or bus terminal. Observation may be possible from some vantage point, but in many instances the only course is to follow the subject under study, and to plot movements on a large-scale plan. Because of the volume of individual movements, sampling will be necessary to avoid any element of prejudice in the selection of persons to be observed or interviewed. It could be every 'n'th person alighting at a bus stop, or passing through a ticket barrier, or crossing some arbitrary line on the pavement. If observation is by following the subject, the surveyor, on returning to the survey point, would wait for a predetermined period and then follow the 'n'th person. No bias will have entered into the selection, and the results can be weighted proportionately to indicate the characteristics of the total movement over certain periods.

A full assessment of movement in an area will be concerned with vehicles and pedestrians, and will involve many of the techniques mentioned. In most instances a considerable number of survey staff will be needed and the handling and processing of data will require a carefully devised office procedure. Surveys of this type can only rarely be undertaken by one individual, but they require one full-time director to control all the various survey and analytical tasks which are involved.

Cost-benefit surveys

The cost of road improvements and new works is high, but to what extent are these costs offset by the gains which accrue to the community through this development?[11] An improvement to a road junction or the creation of a pedestrian precinct or the removal of parked vehicles to an off-the-street site can reduce the number of accidents and increase the speed of vehicular movement. The direct gains can be measured, but depend for their validity on a sequence of surveys over a period of time. In the above illustration it is necessary to know the accident rate and the speed of vehicular movement both before and after the development. The latter factor is usually measured in normal working hours, and may relate to both the 'average' and to the 'peak' speeds of transit over specific routes.

An interesting example of this form of traffic assessment is provided by H. F. Alston's analysis of traffic delays at level crossings in the City of Hull.[12] The daily cost of closures was assessed in vehicle-hours and man-hours of wasted time, and these data were translated into monetary terms by the use of figures on vehicle-operating costs and average hourly earnings. A second illustration is provided by the traffic investigation and economic assessment of the London-Birmingham motorway.[13] The investigation was into the anticipated volumes of traffic, based on surveys of traffic on existing roads with predictions of the amounts which could be expected on the motorway, and the foreseeable economic return in relation to the outlay to be incurred. The study was undertaken after the construction of the motorway had commenced, and would have been of even greater value had the examination been earlier. The scope of the terms of reference should have also been extended to include the *relative* benefits which might result from, say, a London to Birmingham, Birmingham to South Wales, or Liverpool to Leeds motorway. The scope of such studies might indeed be further extended to examine the impact which such roads can be expected to have on the pattern of industrial location, the outward residential movement from towns, and the character of nearby central areas through changes in accessibility.[14]

Within a larger context towns, in contrast to inter-urban areas, suffer from the greatest traffic volumes, the narrowest streets, most road junctions and access points, most parked vehicles, the slowest traffic speeds, and the greatest population densities. It would thus seem that within urban areas a greater cost-benefit can be obtained through road improvements than elsewhere, and this positive factor of greater benefits should be offset against the higher cost of schemes through compensation and disturbance in urban than rural environments. Would a comparative cost-benefit analysis as between the Stretford-Eccles and London-Birmingham motorways confirm this hypothesis and help to usher more urban motorways into the British scene? Or is there more political prestige in the greater lengths of rural motorways for the same cost?

The country expects to spend considerable sums of money as a national investment in a modern highway system. In the words on the London-Birmingham motorway report, 'expenditure on the inquiries described herein can be put at about £20,000. The capital cost of the motorway, however, is estimated to be about £24,000,000. About one-tenth of 1 per cent has thus been spent on inquiries designed to estimate the gains accruing from the investment'.[15] Planned developments, be they urban renewal or the dispersal of population or the lay-out of a residential environment, are expensive procedures; the cost of research is marginal to the total expenditure and will, in the long-term analysis, prove beneficial for the environment to be planned. The argument is not surveys for survey's sake, but to provide the facts on which policy decisions can be based.

The Cumbernauld traffic survey

A traffic study at the New Town of Cumbernauld provides an admirable example of the contribution of traffic surveys within the planning process.[16] The general road plan of the preliminary planning proposals showed an outer ring road serving as a distributor to the housing areas, an inner ring road to provide access to and yet avoid congestion in the town centre, and a separate footpath system. The problems for elucidation were the probable traffic volumes that would occur on the main road network and at the principal junctions. The methods of investigation involved the interpretation of known and anticipated facts, assumptions based on the best available estimates, and assumptions derived from experience elsewhere—albeit rather lacking in basic research studies. It was decided to concentrate the emphasis of the survey upon 'the movement of the working population returning home from work on a typical week-day', i.e. the peak traffic flow of the evening rush hour, and especially of private vehicles.

Assumptions were made initially about the size of the population to be housed in the designated area and the average number of persons per family. It was anticipated that an inward and outward movement of the working population would occur, and assumptions were made about the principal exporting areas, the volume of the inward movement and its distribution over the industrial areas in Cumbernauld. Like calculations were made for the outward daily movement to localities beyond the town. For travel within the town it was assumed that the number of persons employed in each centre would be evenly distributed throughout all residential zones.

From the above facts, and knowing the anticipated densities in each of the smaller areas of the main residential zones, 'work dispersion factors' were calculated, i.e. the number of workers from each housing area employed in each centre. The next stage was to assess how these persons would travel to work. Bicycles were not considered because of the hilly nature of the town and, in determining carriage capacities, one power-assisted cycle was regarded as the equivalent of one car. As the town was planned to receive all sections of the community by varying the type of work, housing densities and the size and rental of houses, a cross-section of the national incomes was expected and assumptions about the car-owning characteristics in 1971 of each income bracket were then made. The distribution of the various income groups about the town was then apportioned on the basis of variations in density and the position of the higher rental accommodation.

It was then assumed that persons within half a mile of their place of work would walk, and assumptions were made about the journey to work of those not walking and having cars. The conclusions thus far were that 20 per cent of the working population would walk, and 28 per cent would travel by car. The remainder would be either passengers in the private vehicles or passengers on public service vehicles. As surveys elsewhere have suggested that there is one passenger for every two vehicles, 14 per cent of the remainder were distributed as car passengers and 38 per cent were allocated to travel in public service vehicles.

The information was now available for a complete breakdown of work journeys according to the origin and destination of workpeople and their mode of travel. Similar methods were applied to people travelling to work in Cumbernauld, and travelling out from Cumbernauld to work. The total volumes of traffic were then considered; information was plotted on the probable routes for each group of vehicles; traffic flow, and the direction and volume of traffic at each junction was then assessed. As a result of these somewhat complex, but nevertheless logical, appreciations the capacity for which roads and junctions should be designed was known. The survey also revealed certain deficiencies in the original road lay-out —thus modifications were required to the road lay-out around the central area to reduce the number of junctions receiving the major traffic flows, and some special provisions were necessary for traffic leaving the town via one of the industrial areas. Changes to the planning proposals necessitated a reappraisal of these survey characteristics, to illustrate the never ending process of continual interaction between survey and plan. The next stage must be to check the validity of findings against the reality of experience. The lessons to be learned on method can then be applied in later studies of the same type. Survey methods, like planning itself, should never attain a finality; the aim must be continually to improve in the accuracy of understanding and in comprehension of the many factors which enter into the problem under study.

This Cumbernauld report suggests the calibre of the methodical survey work which is demanded when the exercise is to design a living environment for a new community of 70,000 persons. It is relatively easy to be wise and critical after the event; the research worker in planning will try to anticipate and to make appropriate provision for future events. When millions of pounds are being spent on roads alone this fundamental approach, with all its difficulties and possible criticisms, is surely justified.

Conclusion

What should be self-evident requires reiteration. No plan for the use and development of land, either at the broad regional scale or at the more intimate levels of detailed design, should ever be prepared without full cognizance of the needs of the moving and standing vehicles. Traffic studies and a full understanding of these requirements must be undertaken at an early stage in the planning process in order to permit the factual and scientifically derived conclusions to be translated into the content of two- and three-dimensional plans. The element of time must also not be forgotten: provision of land will often have to be made now for anticipated traffic conditions a decade or more hence.

The high cost of highways merits these meticulous and methodical traffic and travel surveys which, though expensive, arc infinitesimal relative to the ultimate cost of road construction. It must also be remembered that development patterns for several decades ahead will be determined by evolving highway patterns and their access points. Highways encourage land development just as the development of land throws more traffic on to the present highway system. Traffic studies may have to be undertaken separately from land-use studies, just as this chapter is divorced from its predecessor. A valid analysis of the data cannot proceed very far until the separate findings are integrated into an exposition of their mutual and complementary inter-relationships.[17]

1   Road Research Laboratory, *Summaries of Road Research Notes*, available every two months but limited circulation (unpublished).

2   E. Davies (ed.), *Roads and Their Traffic*, 1960.

3   R. B. Mitchell and C. Rapkin, *Urban Traffic, A Function of Land Use*, 1954. See ref. no. 17 for other American sources.

4   See *Town and Country Planning Textbook*, 1950, pp. 360-1, for a useful classification.

5   C. D. Buchanan, *Car Parking in Central Areas*, Public Works and Municipal Services Congress, November 1954; G. Charlesworth and H. Green, *Parking Surveys*, Roads and Road Construction, 1953, pp.130-4; R. G. Knight, *The Parking Problem: A Digest of Literature*, Road Research Laboratory, Library Communication no. 154, 1950 (unpublished).

6   The official publications are now out-of-date but include R. B. Hounsfield, *Traffic Survey*, 1948; Ministry of Transport, Circular no. 612 and enclosure, *Origin and Destination Surveys of Road Traffic*, H.M.S.O., 1948.

7   W. F. Cassie and J. H. Jones, *The Tyne Tunnel: a Traffic and Economic Study*, Bulletin no. 14, Department of Civil Engineering, University of Durham, 1958.

8   J. C. Tanner, *Some Information Concerning Expenditure on Travel in Different Areas*, Road Research Laboratory, Research Note no. RN/3214/JCT, March 1958 (unpublished).

9   London Transport Executive, *London Travel Survey, 1954*, 1956.

10   F. Yates, *Sampling Methods for Censuses and Surveys*, 1960, p. 43.

11   D. J. Reynolds (Road Research Laboratory), *The Assessment of Priority for Road Improvement*, H.M.S.O., 1960.

12   H. F. Alston, 'Traffic Delays at Level Crossings', *Journal of the Town Planning Institute*, December 1954, pp. 13-15.

13   J. M. Coburn, M. E. Beesley and D. J. Reynolds, *The London–Birmingham Motorway: Traffic and Economics*, Road Research Laboratory, Research Note no. RN/3552/TMC.MEB.DJR, 1959 (unpublished). Follow-up studies include R. F. F. Dawson, *The*

Effect of the London–Birmingham Motorway on the Journey Times and Fuel Consumption of Commercial Vehicles, Road Research Laboratory, RN/3793/RFFD/1960 (unpublished), and, as above for Private Vehicles, RN/3755/RFFD/1960.

14   J. N. Jackson, 'Motorways and Regional Planning', *Journal of the Town Planning Institute,* vol. XLVII, March 1961. For American studies in this field see W. L. Garrison (ed.), *Studies of Highway Development and Geographic Change,* 1959.

15   Coburn, etc., op. cit., p. ii.

16   L. Hugh Wilson, *Cumbernauld New Town, Traffic Analysis Report,* 1958 (unpublished).

17   Major American studies of traffic and land-use relationships include *Detroit Metropolitan Area Traffic Study,* 1955–6; *Transportation Plan: National Capital Region,* 1959; *Nashville Metropolitan Area Transportation Study,* 1961. Future traffic flows between any two localities, forecast from the anticipated land-use and population distributions, are assigned to existing routes to reveal pressures and deficiencies. Alternative highway and transportation proposals are then considered. The ability to direct and control land use (implicit in British planning practice through green belts, new towns, industrial location, density control, etc.) has yet to be reflected in these primarily highway and traffic studies. The work programme of the current *Penn Jersey Transportation Study* may rectify these deficiencies. The intentions (April 1960) were to consider alternative schematic patterns of metropolitan development; to evaluate each in the light of social, economic, political and aesthetic considerations; and to show how land-use patterns might be modified by alternative transportation networks. Land-use and transportation models are discussed in L. Wingo, *Transportation and Urban Land,* 1961, and in a special issue of the *Journal of the American Institute of Planners,* vol. XXV, no. 2, 1959. A good general statement of land-use and traffic inter-relationships is R. B. Mitchell, *Metropolitan Planning for Land Use and Transportation,* U.S. Department of Commerce, 1961.

7

INDUSTRIAL SURVEYS

INDUSTRIAL studies provide a major subject for planning investigations for several reasons. Industries are major users of land; redevelopment projects affect industrial activities, and require special knowledge of the siting and building needs of the disturbed premises. Trends in industrial location exert a powerful impact on the physical form and character of towns; industrial development, at the levels of regional location and local siting, must be integrated with other land uses and the pattern of communications. The propensities for industrial growth or decline react as a powerful determinant of population size, and hence determine the range of service activities; planning suggestions that 'the industrial structure should be diversified' or that 'x acres of land are zoned for industrial development at y' should emerge only from an extensive knowledge of existing conditions within the locality and its region. The background against which land-use planners operate is that control over the *location* of industry is a national responsibility exercised by the Board of Trade, whereas *siting* conditions and details are the responsibility of local planning authorities. The distinction cannot be precise, and clashes between 'industrial' and 'planning' policies persist.[1]

Locational factors and industrial attitude surveys

Industrial surveys, like land use, may be introduced within their historic context. It will be relevant to study the factors which induced each of the local industries to establish themselves in the district. The operative causes may be physical, such as water power to drive machinery, reserves of coal or the presence of minerals for processing. It could be the human element such as the availability of a labour supply, freedom from trade restrictions or a development decision inspired by a director's recreational activities. Economic considerations, such as the decline of a former industry, the routing of a railway or road to change the element of accessibility or the proximity of a consumer market, may have predominated. Any one of these causes, or several together, could have proved decisive.

The distinction between initiating and subsequent factors in industrial location may be important.[2] Industrial development creates its own advantages and establishes a community of interest. The attraction of subsidiary and linked enterprises can be identified. The snowball process of growth with the advent of specialist services such as transport arrangements, financial houses or the processing of waste products must be recognized. Initiating factors are those which ushered an industry into a locality; subsequent factors are those which accrue to an industry after its initial decision to develop, but these in their turn may be initiating factors for later industrial developments. The significance of creating advantages through development is reflected in the self-perpetuating growth of urban regions. Industries beget industries, and industrial growth sponsors the growth of ancillary services—the whole matrix of industrial, commercial, residential and transport development being interconnected and interassociated. Again the concern of the planner is as much with the relationships which exist between different factors as with the factors themselves.

The extent to which the various siting factors are still operative might take the form of an attitude survey among established enterprises to show how firms are carrying on their operations with respect to various factors. One method might be for industrialists to rate predetermined industrial factors as an important advantage, or of little importance, or as a disadvantage of their existing location. Factors might include the adequacy, dependability and cost (as separate subjects) of water, electricity, gas, transport, raw materials and labour, and the attitude of the community. Replies can be tabulated by locality or by industry, and for the factors separately or in combination.

In addition an 'advantage ratio' can be computed. This is simply the number of firms indicating that the factor is an advantage divided by the number that indicated it to be a disadvantage. 'Arranging in this fashion the combined opinions or judgments of responsible industrial officers certainly gives a composite picture of some significance . . . A study of this kind would show the relative strengths and weaknesses of a locality not as seen from outside by prospective newcomers, but as they appear to those who have had actual experience under the conditions existing at the time and place. It would indicate those relative advantages and weak spots of the locality from the point of view of industrial managements in different kinds of enterprises. Thus it could reveal sore points on some of which, perhaps, changes or improvements could be made. This is not to say, of course, that the judgement of the industrialists should dictate public policy, but simply that their estimates of existing conditions might well be considered in the shaping of that policy.'[3]

Another series of meaningful questions will be concerned with the space requirements of present industries. To what extent can these needs be met by more efficient use of the existing buildings, or is expansion on to nearby land (or elsewhere) justified? Direct interview, rather than a postal questionnaire, will yield more reliable results because of the many complexities involved. A statement of land-use needs of existing industry will emerge.

The appraisal of industrial structure

The analysis of statistical data will reveal the relationships of the total numbers in employment to both the total population and the population of working age. The total employment of insured workers engaged in each separate industry may then be indicated in absolute and relative terms to reveal the principal economic activities of the area. These studies gain considerably in value when local conditions can be compared with the regional structure, and regional characteristics with national standards.

Several measures contribute towards this understanding. The West Midland Group used the 'location quotient', the division of the local percentage of all workers in an industry by the comparable national percentage;[4] Isles and Cuthbert have calculated a 'coefficient of divergence' which groups together the excess percentage of industries with a larger percentage share of employment than nationally.[5] The 'location quotient' simplifies comparisons for the purpose of analysis by revealing the relationship between two percentages; when the quotient is above one, then local employment is in excess of the national average and, if less than one, it shows a deficiency in this employment relative to national conditions. The 'index of divergence' shows, for any year for which it is calculated, the percentage of employed workers who would need to be redistributed in order to make the relative sizes of the different industries precisely the same as in the United Kingdom. These measures assist in understanding the nature of the industrial structure and will reveal regional differences. Such understanding should precede the formulation of land-use policies, but should not at this stage imply any qualitative judgement about either specialization or its significance.

Unemployment may arise when either the economy depends on mineral resources, which must by their very nature become exhausted, or on export markets, which can be lost by changes in world trade, or where technological advance or consumer habits make the local product redundant or obsolete. In these circumstances arguments for introducing mobile expanding industries as an insurance against depression may be strong. Further considerations should however be examined, as not all specialized industrial areas have the same need for diversification. Areas serving export rather than home markets tend to fluctuate more violently; the trade cycle is more pronounced in capital-equipment than the consumer-goods industries, in heavy engineering than in food or drink manufacture; within one industry, a variety of different products may provide resilience to the economy as in the metal trades of the Birmingham conurbation. No simple equation exists between over-specialization and the need to diversify the industrial background.

A clue towards understanding the effects of industrial structure on urban growth is the distinction between employment in industries which exist in every community (transport, hospitals, hotels, shops, offices, schools) and industries which are localized or concentrated in certain towns (textile production, motor-car production, universities). This distinction is more fundamental than between service and manufacturing industry. The phrase 'non-basic' (serving local demands) and 'basic' (serving non-local demands) has been much used,[6] but a happier terminology has been introduced by Alexandersson. 'Production for the city's own inhabitants is referred to as "city serving production" . . . Industries which produce for a market outside the geographic city limit . . . are the agglomerative element, the *raison d'être* of the city, and might therefore be termed "city-forming industries". They bring money to the city, which is used to pay for the imports of such goods and services in which the city is deficient.'[7]

The question posed for investigation is 'What ratios in different industries are a necessary minimum to supply a city's own population with goods and services of the type which are produced in every normal city?' The comparison cannot be with the statistical concept of the national average, as it is patently untrue that every town or economic region has a modicum of shipbuilding, textile and chemical industries. This methodological difficulty is overcome by assuming that the town with the *minimum* employment in every industrial activity has sufficient employment to meet the needs of its own population. Any employment additional to this rate can be regarded as being in city-forming industries. The calculation of this minimum ratio for towns of varying size per 1,000 population would exclude 'abnormal' towns and would be based on 'established communities with a reasonable range of economic activities ' (i.e. a new town not yet established and with inhabitants visiting nearby towns for services would be excluded, as would a purely service centre lacking manufacturing industry). The great importance of this concept is the effect which changes in the city-forming industries have on a town's growth or decline. If these industries expand, then a consequential process of growth in the industries serving the greater population results. The principal factor in the process of urban growth will have been isolated and special studies among the city-forming industries may then be undertaken to assess their future potential.

Trends over the past decade may indicate malaise or vigour. Expanding industries may have recognizable signs such as a high proportion of youthful employees, a substantial entry of juveniles, the construction of new buildings and other expansion programmes, while the retirement of older workers is more than offset by the number of new entrants. By contrast in one study of a declining industry, 29 per cent of the males were aged 15–39, compared with 36 per cent in this industry nationally and about 50 per cent of males in all industries in England and Wales; 71 per cent of employed females were aged 40–64. If the age-sex structure of employees was projected forward 10 years, by allowing for retirement and adding to the base the present numbers aged 15–24, then the male labour force would diminish by 24 per cent and the female labour force by 36 per cent.[8] A realistic assessment of industrial prospects, based on studies of the industries concerned and in consultation with trade organizations, must yield fundamental information on industrial prospects to the planning authority. Industrial and associated land-use policies can then be formulated from the basis of the available evidence.

To facilitate comparisons between the industrial characteristics of different employment exchange areas, Isles and Cuthbert used 'a coefficient of industrial density' based on the number of insured workers in each area (excluding agriculture) expressed as a proportion of the total population of the area.[9] This measure has the disadvantage of giving a false impression in areas where people live and do not work or work but not live, but away from the city-commuting areas can result in valuable inferences. Thus the authors observed a wide variation in conditions between different areas: low industrial densities occurred in areas with the smallest population and tended to be most distant from the main centre of employment, and areas with a high density had a smaller proportion of workers in the service industries than did those areas with a low industrial density.

A further element in the industrial structure is the size of firms which reflects itself in different demands for land use and traffic potential. 'Large plants are on the whole associated with high capital investment, especially mechanization';[10] or 'there is a close mutual dependence between the size of firms, the way in which they are organized and financed, and the rate of growth in the total stock of capital'.[11] The size of firms may influence its degree of mobility, and also its suitability for location in different areas. It would usually be wrong to introduce a firm with a large employment potential into a small town, unless growth was required.

Employment is the measure of the industrial characteristics of a locality most used by planners, but other methods (production by weight, cost, value, per man-hour, per unit of horse-power) can measure economic activity. The use of input-output techniques at the local or regional levels would suggest the economic relationships which exist between industries, and the flow of commodities between different localities. Employment may be declining, but through better buildings, improved machinery, automation or changes in management, output or productivity could be increasing. A further point is that, when the percentage employed in an industrial group is declining, this means only that, relative to other employment activities, the industry is of decreasing importance; it can be that the total number employed in this industry is increasing, but that this rate of change is less than that of the town's total employed population.

Employment opportunities

The employment in a locality may be subdivided and analysed in various ways. What is the ratio between employed males and females? How does this vary as between different industries? What are the differences from national and regional standards? Why do these exist and what is their significance for planning policies? Is there the same range of industrial openings for both males and females? What are the trends in male and female employing industries? The important concept of 'concealed unemployment' may be disclosed by these studies, i.e. where the proportion of occupied females in the working age groups is less than the national average, to provide an indication that this number of additional women would be in gainful employment if suitable jobs were available. This measure is usually best on a regional basis, as allowances may otherwise have to be made to allow for the journey to work; thus a large inward movement of males would depress the proportion of females.

At a more local level of study, to what extent are the large employers of female labour dependent upon a labour force living in the immediate vicinity of the works? This dependence may exist for certain groups of married women where there is a tradition of 'working in the factory round the corner', or when an evening shift of married workers is operated. If this home-workplace relationship exists, to what extent does it pose difficulties for slum clearance and dispersal? Is it an argument for high densities upon redevelopment, or does it suggest the need for female-employing industries in or near new residential areas?

Another important subject is the entry of juveniles into employment. When there are local deficiencies, then the emigration of this group of workers may be encouraged. The Youth Employment Officer can provide information on the number of placings, but the data refer mainly to secondary modern and technical schools and include few grammar-school leavers. It is not therefore comprehensive but, even so, may suggest deficiencies in the local economy. Are there enough local openings with apprentice schemes for the pupils classified as 'technically skilled'? Is there any down-grading of school-leavers through the paucity of local skilled opportunities, or the enforced entry of school-leavers into posts of less than their occupational ability? Are there sufficient opportunities for advancement locally? Do the conclusions apply with equal validity to boys and girls? The future number of people entering the working age groups each year may be calculated from tables giving the number of persons aged 0–21 by individual ages in the Census of Population. The impact of the 'bulge' of school-leavers passing from primary to secondary schools and thence into industry has been foreseen since 1950 as part of an inevitable natural process which should be planned for.

Another significant criterion of well-being in the employment structure is status in employment. The Census of Population has been seen to provide certain broad information whereby this factor may be compared as between different localities. A further source, though now more of historical than direct relevance, is the comparison between parts A and B of the employment exchange returns of insured persons at mid-1948. Part A listed persons who had contributed previously to unemployment insurance and part B those who were entering insurance for the first time (including non-manual workers earning over £420 p.a.), so as to provide some measure of the quality of occupations in a locality. The proportion of new males then entering insurance provides some index of the jobs which might be described as the 'most desirable'. This aspect of employment may be studied for the main employment groups, and relative to the national conditions in that industry and·for all industrial groups. A lack of opportunity reflects a local deficiency, which may in its turn contribute towards emigration in search of better opportunities.

Over-specialization, deficiencies in male or female employment, limited openings for juveniles or inadequate opportunities for advancement may justify the attraction of new industrial development. The national criterion of need is, however, high relative unemployment, and hence the study of unemployment, a topic important in itself, attains a special significance. The first points for elucidation are the total numbers of males and females unemployed, their industrial groups and length of unemployment. Is the locality prone to severe fluctuations and, if so, which industrial groups are the first to be affected and how long does the depression take to spread to the city-serving industries? Trends in unemployment over a period of time should be related to the total number of occupied persons, rather than to the total population, in order to exclude different proportions of children, retired or otherwise not employed persons. A study of long-term and seasonal unemployment trends in the major industrial groups would also be appropriate, and comparisons, as with the previous data, should be made with regional and national conditions.

Unemployment affects the whole well-being of a town, its range of services, its vitality and its trends of total population. Planners must therefore appreciate the operative causes and approach remedial policies at a regional scale. The location of an industrial estate or the attractive power of access points on a new motorway for industrial location may provide sufficient inducements to reverse the trends. Alternatively the approach might be extensive landscape improvement to make the locality more attractive. It may also be to encourage the element of job mobility, the movement of persons from town to town or between regions in search of better employment opportunities. It should not be axiomatic that a high level of unemployment merits a policy of industrial attraction; there are many other planning elements for consideration and a rigid pursuit of the policy of 'work to the workers' endorses the nineteenth-century pattern of industrial distribution in a period of changing technology and needs.

It is also wrong to equate a substantial volume of daily journey to work with a need for industrial development, as the problem may not have industrial implications. If x workers travel from A to B, then x (or $\frac{x}{2}$) jobs should not necessarily be provided in A. This approach might disrupt the economy of B; it ignores the fact that some element of inter-urban movement is essential for the efficient functioning of the economy, that many commuters travel because of other factors such as a wish for a house near the country, and that the greater distance of travel (e.g. by fast train) may be less irksome than a shorter (e.g. cross-town) journey. The research worker should establish not only the volume of movement but, more important, the attitudes to travel. Sample surveys by interview, in residential areas, for places of work, mode and cost of travel and attitude to the journey and in workplaces for times of arrival and departure, will be more pertinent as a basis for policies to relieve congestion. The problem may be closer to traffic planning than industrial location.

An understanding of the relationships between home and workplace may also be significant in slum clearance projects. In addition to married women, certain groups of male workers may be tied to living in certain localities, for instance people working to times other than the normal bus schedules (shift workers, persons starting early in the morning or finishing late at night), low income groups, elderly and infirm workers, casual labour and unskilled workers, and persons in dirty or wet jobs which may make travel particularly unpleasant.[12] Again the study is of personal needs and preferences.

The conclusions may influence the density of redevelopment, or the location of new development relative to the major industrial areas.

Population projections and industrial policy

The relationship between future population and the required number of work-places is complex. Present statistics refer to the number of workers insured against unemployment, and would change overnight if the age of retirement or school-leaving age were altered. No amount of survey can anticipate these possibilities. A second difficulty is that the number of workers will depend on the success of industrial policies, and this in its turn may hinge upon the construction of a motorway, the augmentation of a water supply, the achievement of a dozen such developments, or a political act of faith. A failure to encourage industrial development in a declining town may sponsor emigration, whereas smoke control, landscape reclamation and the fortuitous expansion of a local industry might induce the return of former migrants. In view of these uncertainties and the mutual interaction of different development decisions, an appropriate method is to investigate the effects which are likely to occur in the size of the present working population through the agencies of natural change, the migration of potential labour supplies, and through changes in the composition of the population.

The first component depends on the entry into employment of juveniles and others seeking employment for the first time, and the reduction in employment by retirement, death, sickness, disablement or marriage (women only). The Census of Population provides data for the composition of the working age groups in five-yearly intervals. In five years' time the upper layer will retire, deaths will deplete the number of persons in each of the other working groups and the 10–14-year-olds will reach employment age. Refinements to this broad method of approach will be necessary because the number of insured workers is less than the population of working age, not all juveniles enter employment and others delay their entry to a later age, and older workers may leave work before reaching retirement age.

These individual components are not known but one composite adjustment, which assumes that rates of entry and departure remain unchanged, will suffice. Alternatively an allowance could be introduced for a factor such as the raising of the school-leaving age. The method is to express the number of insured males and females as percentages of the male and female persons of working age, and apply these percentages to the net increase in the population of working age. 'In this way full allowance is made for all the variables. . . . Any increase (or decrease) in the labour force due to causes other than the natural increase in the population will show itself, in the year in which it occurs, in an increase (or decrease) in the proportion of insured workers to the population of working age.'[13]

This translation of anticipated trends in the size of the population of working age into an estimate of the number of male and female employees may be made with equal validity for towns or economic regions. The projection can be made for a period of 15 years from the census and beyond this period by making assumptions about the birth rate; on the other hand, longer-term forecasts have little practical usefulness because of the unknown and unincluded factor of migration. On the basis of this projection the natural increase in the male and female labour force is known for some time into the future. The immediate and anticipated needs for jobs can be stated, and these forecasts can be compared with past tendencies. A further factor must now enter the assessment. The forecast is of an increase over the existing numbers in employment. If a decline in employment is anticipated for any industrial group, then the demand for additional employment will be that much greater. The demand is for additional *employment*; this can be through the expansion of existing opportunities, in service industry or by the introduction of new industrial concerns.

School and employment needs in an expanding town

The difference between anticipated labour force and the actual number of jobs will be changed through migration. One special case, with its impact on both educational and employment needs, will be considered—namely the movement of population to new towns and overspill reception areas. The principal population characteristic is the youthful age structure and, in one overspill area, 46 per cent of the new population were children under 15 years of age and 45 per cent were young adults aged 20–39. Only 5 per cent of the immigrants were aged 45 years or over. 90 per cent of families had one or more children of school age or younger, 2 per cent of families had children who were all aged sixteen years or over, and there were 8 per cent of families with no children. The mean family size was 3·9 persons.[14] The overspill population was thus composed primarily of children and of young adults equally apportioned between the sexes. This age concentration and resultant high birth rate is typical of these communities, and is in sharp contrast with the national average.

The first pressure is for schools. The normal method for estimating future school requirements relies on the basis that, for every 1,000 persons, there would be about 14 school-children in each year of age. A neighbourhood unit housing 10,000 persons would thus require, at 40 pupils per class, schools providing 3·5 forms entry. These details may then be translated into site requirements on the basis of the current prescribed Ministry of Education standards for school buildings. By contrast in the above illustration the estate contained an average of about 30 persons at each year of age from 0–14, so the total demand for educational space was at about twice the national level. For every school needed normally, two would be required to meet overspill requirements with consequent implications upon the allocation of land uses, the pattern of physical development on the estates, and the cost of rate-borne services of the receiving authority; a grant towards the cost of the house does not defray the extra expenditure on schools. A further complication may be the division of children between state and denominational schools, through the immigration of Catholic families.

The migration of families creates an immediate demand for placings in primary schools, and a foreseeable pressure for space in the secondary schools. The move of pupils into secondary schools does not, however, diminish the pressure for space at the primary level, because of the high proportion of young children and the high birth rates which are prevalent. Nor will the demand be only ephemeral because the 0–4 generation of immigrants will themselves be of marriageable age in some 15 years, and second generation children will continue to expose an overspill reception area to a higher than national demand for educational places.

Turner, who has studied these educational aspects of an overspill movement, concluded that 'so far as primary school-children are concerned, three features stand out as significant . . . In the first place the number of children in Newtown exceed those in Normtown throughout the whole of the period 1958–98, so the provision of schools on the basis of national figures will fall far short of the demand for school places. Secondly, there is a general upward trend in the number of pupils in Normtown due to the higher post-war birth rate. Finally, the figures for Newtown . . . rise to a peak around 1963, sink to the bottom of a trough in 1978 and rise again to a peak in 1993.'[15] These fluctuations suggest either the use of temporary buildings for educational purposes, or designing to meet the full need and the possibility of reducing class sizes when the supply of pupils is less than the provision of facilities. The provision of primary schools is reflected immediately upon the allocation of land within the residential areas. The problem of secondary education, sited to serve more than one residential area, presents a land-use problem for the greater urban environment.

The age distribution of the overspill population will advance inexorably through the need for educational facilities to the province of the Youth Employment Officer. Within 15 years all the 46 per cent of children aged 0–14 (less a few deaths) will join the working age groups, and over the same period about 2 per cent of the present overspill population will reach pensionable age. The population of working age will thus nearly double over a 15-year period. This rate of growth is striking. It arises solely from the age characteristics of the immigrant population.

The problem of providing adequate employment is not a short-term expedient, but a long-term investment. The average male adult householder has 30–40 years of working life before him, and his youthful family may wish to spend the full 50 years of their working life in the new environment. The attraction of an overspill population cannot be regarded solely, or even primarily, as a housing problem. The allocation of a housing tenancy is merely the first stage in an involved chain of cause and effect. A whole series of related repercussions have been set in motion which influence the use and development of land. The challenge for planning is to show how far these events can be foreseen through the appropriate surveys and intelligent anticipation, and then on the basis of this evidence whether the appropriate land-use provision can be made. Planning 'should not only inquire how this of today may have come out of that of yesterday, but be foreseeing and preparing for what the morrow is even now in its turn bringing towards birth'.[16]

Land for industrial development and industrial mobility

If land is to be allocated for industrial development then the justification will normally be for one or more of four purposes revealed by the various industrial employment or population surveys: the expansion requirements of existing industry on adjacent or other land; the resiting of existing industry which is cramped, badly accommodated or affected by other planning proposals; the resiting of non-conforming industry, though this element tends to be wishful thinking unless the scale of operations is small or the industry is expanding or otherwise wishes to resite itself; the establishment of new industry justified by the anticipated growth in the size of the working population or where the industrial economy requires strengthening for the many factors mentioned above.[17]

Information is now required on the factors influencing industrial location and movement. Surveys may be appropriate to understand why firms have moved and what factors are involved in the selection of new sites? Which firms in the area might be induced to move? Have firms been deterred from establishing themselves in an area? Have firms moved away from an area and, if so, why? The types of survey envisaged will be clear from the framing of the questions. New firms in the district will be studied by attitude surveys, as already suggested, to appreciate why the plants have moved and to understand the importance of various factors which were involved in the selection of new sites. 'Before' and 'after' studies of firms which have moved into a flatted factory or a disused mill or on to a new industrial estate must be undertaken so that the lessons to be learned from this industrial experience can be applied to the reality of the design for the next development project. Knowledge will be required about the linkages of firms and the extent to which they are tied to a locality; such surveys will be essential in clearance areas where the firms will be obliged to vacate their present premises and will be desirable among non-conforming industries. Special investigations may substantiate the contributions which flatted factories can make towards the problem of disturbing many small industries in the redevelopment process.

A revealing survey is of the factors which have *prevented* firms from establishing in a locality. Local industrialists may have offered land for sale only at excessive values, or be in opposition to newcomers 'poaching' on the limited supplies of labour. The reasons may be the availability of water supplies, delays in the national financial approval for the construction of new buildings or roads, or a greater local enthusiasm or trading advantages for development elsewhere. A planning authority able to understand these reasons is in a stronger position to remedy the deficiencies revealed. A comparable investigation is among firms which have closed down a branch factory and moved elsewhere. Why? A methodological difficulty is the complete listing of such firms, though details can be gleaned through the comparison of directories, local knowledge and with the co-operation of the postal authorities.

Special studies of industrial movement in blighted areas may provide significant details. The buildings may be obsolete, the structures in need of repair and traffic circulation inadequate. The tendency may be for certain types of establishment to move outwards with the movement of population; other firms will move into the vacated premises either because of their cheapness or through their locational advantages within the inner ring; yet again other firms may undertake minor changes of location to improve their working conditions. The result will be to obtain a cumulative picture of land-use change among industrial premises in a special type of problem area. The pattern will not be the simple one of decline, but may involve the factors of decentralization, concentration and relocation.

When the clearance of such areas is proposed, there is the moral obligation on planning authorities to provide alternative accommodation for displaced firms and this requires programming elsewhere to minimize dislocation.

Another special problem for land-use planning is provided by the industrial character and trends of industry in small country towns.[18] The subjects for investigation may be the same as already discussed, though more intimate considerations may operate. Thus the importance of personal relationships within the firm, and the local attitude to development, may attain a greater significance. The local transport facilities may mitigate a shift system of working, or be uneconomic to provide for the smaller firms. The absence of facilities for technical training, or an unwillingness to provide a few houses for key workers, may be major obstacles to development. Agricultural interests may oppose industrial location, because of its possible attraction of agricultural labour despite the current loss of this labour to more distant towns, and there is always the 'danger' that a new enterprise will outgrow the needs of a locality and transform its character.

When land is allocated for development some generalized distinction of its suitability for light, heavy or noxious industry may be given. Some further form of categorization might be appropriate. Density considerations can be expressed in terms of 'workers per acre' and may grade from sites for extensive industries, which use large areas of land but with low ratios of persons per acre, to their intensive counterparts where production is concentrated in multi-storey buildings. 'Performance standards' and 'locational needs' may also be emphasized. A series of tests might be applied to determine whether the industry is suitable for inclusion in various parts of the industrial zone(s) by reason of its land and public utility requirements, labour needs, traffic flows, and degree of nuisance through dirt, fumes or noise. Land with railway facilities might be reserved for manufacturers requiring this facility, and land near residential areas for firms employing married women. Land-use control over the location and siting of industry demands a far more comprehensive vision than just the visual and access requirements.

With the need for industry established and the land zoned and available for its reception, there still remains the exacting hurdle of attracting the appropriate type of firm. Certain studies have suggested, for example, the types of firms which might be attracted into a rural environment or the declining textile area of North-East Lancashire.[19] The ability to attract firms will depend in part on the compilation and publicity value of a resource survey with full details of the local availability of minerals, mineral products, partly processed and finished products, public utilities, sites, labour supply, transportation facilities, availability of houses for key workers, social and recreational facilities and so on.[20] In the final analysis, advertising, the pressure which can be exerted by local and national leaders, the offer of inducements through grants and priorities, and the element of sheer luck will all play their part. The prediction of future industrial movements and trends can never be reduced to an exact science.

Recognizing the basic importance of industry to the well-being of their localities, several local authorities have appointed industrial development officers to undertake the various negotiations and to provide liaison between new enterprises and the departments of local government. This responsibility for the implementation of planning proposals should not require the creation of a separate department, because the planning surveys contain all the information required by industrialists. The surveys suggested above are designed to understand the employment and industrial characteristics and potential of the community; their purpose is to propose appropriate planning policies and then to achieve the required development. Implementation is part of the planning process, and should not in this instance be delegated for consideration by a different technical officer and lay committee.

Conclusion

The sequence of repercussions from industrial development has long been recognized. 'When an industry has chosen a locality for itself, it is likely to stay there long, so great are the advantages which people following the same skilled trade get from near neighbourhood to one another. . . . And presently subsidiary trades grow up in the neighbourhood, supplying it with implements and materials, organizing its traffic, and in many ways conducing to the economy of its material.'[21] An understanding of these economic relationships and of the interconnections between industrial activity and the broader urban or regional environments will assist in the identification of those economic activities which sponsor further land-use change. One function of industrial surveys is to indicate the amount, location and type of land and services which will be needed to allow for the achievement and maintenance of full and varied employment both now and during the successive stages of implementing the development plan. When the needs have been established from the study of all industrial and employment characteristics, surveys will then be concerned with establishing the practicability of providing these services and the required number of jobs. These planning studies should operate at the urban, regional and local levels as a prelude to consistent policies integrated with the development of transport, public utility, housing and other services.

1   J. N. Jackson, 'The Location of Industry: Unemployment as the Basis for National Policy', *Town Planning Review*, vol. XXX, no. 3, 1960.

2   J. H. Jones, *A Memorandum on the Location of Industry* in Royal Commission on the Distribution of the Industrial Population, Cmd 6153, 1940, pp. 249–80. See also R. C. Estall and R. O. Buchanan, *Industrial Activity and Economic Geography*, 1961.

3   C. Woodbury (ed.), *The Future of Cities and Urban Redevelopment*, 1955, pp. 138–9.

4   West Midland Group, *Conurbation*, 1948, ch. VIII.

5   K. S. Isles and N. Cuthbert, *An Economic Survey of Northern Ireland*, H.M.S.O., 1957, pp. 123–4.

6   See H. M. Mayer and C. F. Kohn (eds.), *Readings in Urban Geography*, pp. 85–126, for various papers in this theme.

7   G. Alexandersson, *The Industrial Structure of American Cities*, 1956, p.15. The words town and city are used as synonyms.

8   J. N. Jackson, *The Population and Industrial Structure of Macclesfield*, 1960 (unpublished Ph.D. thesis, University of Manchester).

9   Isles and Cuthbert, op. cit., pp. 109–10.

10 P. S. Florence, *Investment, Location and Size of Plant*, 1948, p. 13.

11 Isles and Cuthbert, op. cit., p. 115.

12 Jackson, op. cit.

13 Isles and Cuthbert, op. cit.

14 Jackson, op. cit.

15 R. Turner, *Expanding Towns*, 1959, pp. 56–7 (unpublished Diploma thesis, Department of Town and Country Planning, University of Manchester).

16 Patrick Geddes, *Cities in Evolution*, 1949, p.1.

17 Ministry of Housing and Local Government, *The Use of Land for Industry*, Technical Memorandum no. 2, pp. 13–20 (unpublished).

18 A. Beecham, *Survey of Industries in Welsh Country Towns*, 1951; T. Eastwood, *Industry in the Country Towns of Norfolk and Suffolk*, 1951; T. Thomas and K. S. Woods, *Country Town Industries of South-West England*, Agricultural Economics Research Institute, 1957.

19 P. S. Florence and C. Williams, 'The Selection of Industries suitable for Dispersion into Rural Areas', *Journal of the Royal Statistical Society*, vol. CVII, pt. II, 1945. The Economist Intelligence Unit, *A Study for the Prospects for the Economic Development of North-East Lancashire*, 1959.

20 A full list is included in G. J. R. Linge, *The Future Work-Force of Canberra*, National Capital Development Commission, 1960.

21 A. Marshall, *Principles of Economics*, 8th edition, 1959, p. 225.

POPULATION AND SOCIAL SURVEYS

'THE population basis of a plan cannot be treated conclusively . . . in one section of the Report of Survey . . . Many other chapters will need population statistics to explain changes proposed in land provisions. As these land provisions are designed to meet the various needs of those who use the land, consideration of quantities of land and of population can never be divorced from one another.'[1] Specific studies of population should include an assessment of population size now and as anticipated as a broad guide to the overall land-use needs of the physical environment, the consideration of population composition because of the impact of particular age and household requirements on the provision of land use, and an understanding of population distributions and densities to permit the appropriate allocation of spatial needs throughout the region and within the urban area. Finally, and by no means least, if the phrase 'planning is for people' is to have any validity, then individual and group needs, attitudes and preferences must be understood. Perhaps the greatest failure of British planning is the distinction between the planner and the planned, between 'they' and 'we'. If the interest for planning stems from the people with roots in an area, this will act as a tremendous source of revitalization and of inspiration.

Population distribution, structure and characteristics[2]

Patterns of population distribution can be plotted from statistical series and from maps of settlement to distinguish between various areas of concentration. In a rural area to what extent can the discerned pattern be related to land fertility, residential pressure from the towns, the types of farming, the pattern of communications, or access? Are there any apparent anomalies in this distribution such as fertile areas with a low population? If so, what are the causes, and are planning policies necessary to rectify the observed deficiencies? The types of question will vary according to the terrain and the quality of data; the purpose of phrasing questions is to establish the existence of relationships. Present distributions however represent a growth from the past, and reflect conditions only at one transient point in time. A study of trends and of future possibilities will introduce the significant dynamic element into the appraisal of population characteristics. As with traffic, industry or land use, the concept of changes in time is fundamental to the planning appreciation of the problems involved or emerging.

The continuing interpretation of the population statistics described in Chapter 2 will reveal the changing characteristics of the community. The trends in the total population will reflect the sum total of conditions in the town or the region's basic and service industries, and local characteristics should be compared with the average for England and Wales so that the observed details can be appreciated in their national perspective.

Trends for males and females should be observed separately; the facts may be presented in absolute terms, but each sex can also be studied as a percentage of the total population; changes in these relative proportions may suggest differential migration. The sex ratio of females per 1,000 males by five-year age groups may also be revealing of the same characteristics, and may mirror the availability of employment opportunities.[3] Age distribution is more important than the distribution of the sexes: it is conventionally represented as a pyramid with the youngest and largest age groups at the base, and the width of each layer of the pyramid proportional to the numbers in each age group. The data are available from the census volumes in five-year age groups. The changing pattern of this 'pyramid' in time or between different localities is suggestive of different impacts through changes in the birth rate, greater longevity and migration. The population structures of a New Town, market town and resort are very different and, within a city, substantial differences exist as between declining inner area, inter-war local authority housing areas, and post-war private suburban development. These differences in age composition re-emerge in varying land demands for schools, old people's homes and employment opportunities—three factors which each bear a direct relationship to the age distribution of the population.

Trends within the major age groups may be examined by dividing the population into a working section and those who, because they are either too old to work or too young, remain dependent on those of working age. Subgroups of the dependent section include children aged 0–14 and retired persons, males aged 65 and over and women aged 60 and over. Admittedly the division into precise groups is arbitrary, but trends should be viewed against the background of the national norm, and in their impact on land-use requirements. Further refinements can be introduced as required, such as between the younger and older working age groups or between the children of primary- and secondary-school age.

Family size and housing needs

Marriage and family considerations should now be taken into account. It is necessary to distinguish between non-private and private households, and to study their trends separately. The siting or growth of an institution can change a population in decline to one of apparent expansion and of immigration, and conceal the reality of emigration.

The size of families, or rather the number of persons per private household, provides a potent element in the physical size of communities and its demands for housing space. Almost everywhere the demand for houses, as represented by the number of separate households, is relatively greater than changes in the total population size. The physical enlargement of towns by the addition of pre- and post-war residential estates is made possible by the motor-car, but can be explained more by considerations of family size than through changes in the size of the total population. Had this factor been appreciated fully when the first development plans were prepared in 1951, then the allocation of land for residential and ancillray purposes would have been more realistic than has proved to be the case.

The principal explanations of the decline in household size are the ageing of the population, already noted, and the fall in the birth rate through the use of birth-control methods. A useful index to show this latter trend is the general fertility rate, which may be compiled direct from the census returns by dividing the number of young children aged 0–4 by the number of women in the child-bearing age groups (15–49).

The average size of families conceals more detailed information upon the distribution of private households by their size. The data may be presented either in the form of the number (or percentage) of households containing the stated number of persons, or in the terms of the population in households with the stated number of persons; thus x per cent of households have three persons, or y per cent of the population live in three-person households. The concepts are rather different, and an understanding of their changing nature results in an appreciation of the importance of household formation in the assessment of housing need.[3]

A further element in housing demand is the marital status and age of the heads of private households, which emerges from a new tabulation in the 1951 Census of Population. The need for accommodation depends, at least in part, on whether these households are growing, stationary or declining. Ford and Thomas have suggested that expanding families comprise those family units with a married head of the household aged under 40 and with three or less dependants; stationary families are those with a married head of the household either aged under 40 and with four or more dependants, or aged between 40–59 or aged 60 and over with three or less dependants, or aged 60 and over when the household unit contains only one or two persons; declining families are those with either a married head aged 40–59 and with four or more children, or with a married head over 60 and with more than one dependant; within the non-married groups aged 40–59 and 60 and over, half of each of the family groups are regarded as stationary and half as declining; heads with bachelors or spinsters under 40 are regarded as stationary rr espective of the number of persons.[4]

The next stage, with the numbers in each of these categories having been deduced either from the census for the town as a whole or by a survey in clearance projects, is to translate these characteristics of family structure into terms of rooms. A standard allocation of one habitable room per person cannot be applied universally without prior sample surveys because this may bear no relation to the way in which households occupy their dwellings— e.g. the use of communal rooms, how the bedrooms are shared or the segregation of the sexes. The criteria and assumptions used by Ford and Thomas were that married couples share a bedroom; in half the households all other persons are given a separate bedroom and in the other half sufficient bedrooms are provided to segregate all other persons by sex; all expanding households are given an extra bedroom; one-fifth of the stationary and declining households consisting of childless married couples are also allowed an extra bedroom; all households, with the exception of 50 per cent of the stationary and declining single person households, are given a living-room in addition to the bedroom.[5] The resultant tabulation is of the size of houses required for all private households by their number of rooms. The methods can be applied with equal validity to the size of houses required by all households within a slum clearance programme.

Social surveys of housing needs and attitudes

A full appreciation of housing needs would assess the total of replacements made necessary by the demolition of substandard dwellings, in the process of developments such as road widening or central area expansion, by the removal of temporary dwellings and by conversions to other uses. Needs additional to the present stock of dwellings would arise through overcrowding in existing dwellings and population factors such as natural change, migration and household formation. Sites must then be selected. The physical choice lies between the redevelopment of cleared sites or the development of vacant sites in the city, on the rural-urban fringe, in towns beyond the city or in new centres. In each instance a variety of different densities and forms of layout are possible, but in addition to the many physical, economic and aesthetic factors involved in these considerations, social surveys can contribute much useful information about the needs of people to be housed and the attitudes of people who have been rehoused. Public attitudes and preferences act as a powerful determinant over the use and development of land, and an understanding of these forces will enable the development plan to accord with (or to oppose through the more powerful operation of some other factor or group of factors) the concepts of the people living, working or otherwise using an area. Social surveys can be conducted in many fields other than housing; housing merely provides a convenient milieu for discussion.

Slum clearance emerges as a housing problem resulting from physical decay and obsolescence, but the effects are on people and families. It is the very element of compulsion in the move, through the undoubted need to redevelop great tracts of our inner urban areas, which makes understanding and knowledge of the human problem so essential. 'One thing is clear, that in carrying out their slum clearance proposals local authorities will be called on to think out a large number of personal problems that affect the offer of a house: the type of accommodation, its location, the rent to be charged, its position in relation to old friends and new neighbours. Not the least important part of the long process of slum clearance is the careful study of the needs of individual families and the search for ways of meeting them.'[6]

The distinction between social surveys of needs and of attitudes is important. The needs of people in a clearance area can be translated into terms of physical action such as the need for 'x' two-bedroomed houses or, more meaningful, for 'a' two-bedroomed houses in this location and for 'b' two-bedroomed houses in that location. These preferences can be stated as between the range of possible choices (inner area house, terrace house in a suburb, etc.) and will emerge from a variety of family circumstances including journey to work, the pull of the extended family, family size, income, religious affiliations, club membership and other personal factors. Such surveys should not be restricted to families in the dwellings to be cleared, but must involve other groups such as small industrialists; the element of choice may here range between a flatted factory or a small building in two or three alternative situations. The owners and tenants of shops, the authorities responsible for institutions such as schools, churches, clubs and public houses, will all have their differing needs.

Attitudes within a redevelopment area will be many and varied. There will be no such thing as a prevailing attitude, and the planning function is rather to understand the views, preferences and prejudices of the many different groups which exist. The range of opinion is as important as the majority or typical attitudes. Residential groups may include tenants and owner-occupiers, families sharing accommodation and those occupying separate dwellings, families where only the male householder works and those with both husband and wife (perhaps also children) in employment, families in different types of dwelling by size or condition or proximity to environmental nuisances, persons of different age or education, families of different size or with varying lengths of residence or with varying degrees of attachment to churches and social institutions, wage earners in different occupations or with different places and hours of work, and families with different household incomes and paying differing amounts for their accommodation. Each of these factors will influence attitudes, and any one person or family will of course be influenced by more than one of these several groups. The diversity of attitudes must be cross-tabulated against the various characteristics to permit a full analysis of the situation. Social accounting, the listing of all the various elements in the situation, must be followed by an assessment of the impact of each element upon development policies.

It is important to stress that an attitude survey towards a *new* environment cannot be undertaken in an old area. No amount of questioning can reveal the response of families towards dispersal or towards living in tall blocks of flats unless the conditions have been experienced. Surveys can however be undertaken in overspill reception areas and in high density redevelopment projects to assess attitudes to the internal layout of the dwelling, its external space relationships, its position relative to shopping and public open space, the adequacy of environmental facilities including shops and schools, and the effect of the move upon family ties and journey to work. If the social characteristics of the population in these new areas can be compared with the population in the old areas, or if a sequence of 'before' and 'after' studies of the same group in its old and new environments can be undertaken, then valid deductions can result in an appreciation of the effect of these changes on individual and family life. Many new housing and overspill developments are described as 'experiments' or 'pilot schemes'; surely the essence of an experiment is to learn from observation and study of the results. Surveys can also be undertaken among the 'disgruntled element' who have returned to their former living environment. Are the reasons for this apparent 'failure' remediable? Are any particular groups involved?

These investigations must be broadly conceived, otherwise an undue emphasis on any one factor may stress that one consideration to the exclusion of other elements. Thus Vereker and Mays have commented critically on the mainly historical approach of sociologists in that 'decisions framed primarily in terms of what has been the case in the past without regard to possible changes could prove as ill-founded as those reached without close attention to the existing situation and the factors responsible for its occurrence'.[7] These arguments derive from a study of social characteristics in an inner area of Liverpool. 'During the early days of the research it was assumed too readily that the past invariably spoke for the future and that rooted families would wish to remain where they had existed for more than one generation. But when the subdivisions were scrutinized in terms of the respondents' desire to move away, it was discovered that the wards which had proved most stable in the past contained the highest proportion of people wishing to move in the future . . . In short, indices of past stability are no sure guarantee against future mobility.' The strong pull of family tie exists in many clearance localities.

Studies in new areas show that separation from relatives can create dissatisfaction, but there is also a considerable body of evidence to show that the joys and pleasures of a new house in a decent environment outweigh these family disadvantages. Persons who have returned back to older areas have done so, in the main,

because of difficulties either in employment or through the social
and economic hardships of an enforced journey to work. Social
surveys with conclusions for planning should see the variety of
elements involved in perspective, and relative to the operation of
other factors, rather than in isolation.

The need for social surveys within the planning process has been
ably stated by Catherine Bauer. 'The fact is that every aspect of
housing and city planning policy comes down, sooner or later, to
qualitative social decisions, value judgements about individual needs
and preferences, family and community functions, group relations,
and the whole pattern of civic life. Such judgements are peculiarly
difficult to make in a society as varied and changing as ours, but they
will nevertheless affect our everyday life for generations to come . . .
the planner wants to know the scientific effect of a particular factor
in environment over which he has some *bona fide* control, and the
interrelation between one factor and another. Also, he needs to know
what to do, not merely what to avoid. . . . He is interested in the
social effect of the kind of environment produced, or capable of
being produced, today. . . . The geographic relationship of homes to
employment, schools, shops and leisure-time pursuits calls for social
investigations beyond the mere measurement of traffic flow. . . .
Research should distinguish between average behaviour and
attitudes under *status quo* conditions, and emerging trends in social
values and activities . . . What we really need to know therefore is
what people would want if they understood the full range of
possibility on the one hand, and all the practical limitations on the
other.'[8]

Social surveys and citizen participation

Social surveys also have the important function of stimulating the
community into positive action. The phrase 'citizen participation'
has yet to cross the Atlantic as a potent force within planning,
though perhaps the mushroom growth of Amenity Societies through
the work of the Civic Trust is a pointer to the possibilities. Local
knowledge, initiative and enthusiasm can achieve much, and the
attraction of private capital into redevelopment is essential if the

speed of urban renewal is to be advanced. 'If or when the more drastic clearance and rebuilding forms of redevelopment reach the scale they should attain, they will do more to upset patterns of living, to unsettle established groups and their complex personal relationships, and to disturb institutions and organizations than any other single activity. . . . It is unthinkable that this kind of programme can be vigorously pushed for long without substantial and widespread understanding and support among many of the major groups that make up our cities. It is almost equally difficult to believe that such an operation can yield the optimum balance of benefits over costs and hardships unless many of these groups have some voice in determining what is to be done and when.'[9]

The need for redevelopment through physical, structural and environmental obsolescence can hardly be doubted; one challenge before British planning is the extent to which public opinion can be harnessed to technical know-how to achieve through mutual cooperation and endeavour a better environment. 'If more than lipservice is to be given to the phrase "planning is for people", then redevelopment should become a process in which people can take some part: not just a few carefully selected or self-appointed persons but many, if possible, a larger proportion of the ordinary people of the community . . . A programme in which the citizen can participate in the planning process and in fact influence, to a substantial extent, the way in which his area will be developed is an overwhelming need.'[10] Social surveys, and social scientists, have much to contribute within this field of technical and lay co-operation. The contact between officials and people at the interview stage is initially to obtain information, but also fosters good relationships through personal contact and discussion of the range of possibilities. Planning requires good will, and this should never be dissipated.

Which British cities have anything comparable to Philadelphia's 'Citizens' Council on City Planning'? Their annual report for 1960–1 is introduced by the phrase, 'In Philadelphia the Citizen Participates in Planning.' It describes downtown luncheon meetings on 'planning subjects of city-wide interest'; it states that 'at the *request* of Philadelphia's city council, our Transportation Committee has undertaken a very comprehensive study with a view toward evolving an over-all long-term transit and transportation policy for the City'. The function of the Citizens' Council is to bring 'to governmental agencies the aspirations and reactions of the citizens; and conversely, it assists these agencies in informing the public as to the complex planning issues with which government is concerned'.[11]

The concentration of shop and office employment in congested central areas may be used in illustration of this theme for enthusiasm to achieve planned development. The staggering of working hours might be thought to provide one solution to this problem, and a survey of the starting and departure times of employees firm by firm will yield the requisite information about traffic generated at short regular periods throughout the rush hour.[12] The degree to which established offices might be willing to disperse to outlying centres and thus ease the situation could also be ascertained through valid surveys. The successful pursuit of either policy will depend upon an enthusiastic approach from the planners *and* the planned. Surveys will provide initial data to show whether the policy is feasible. This evidence will then be discussed with the appropriate commercial interests as a basis for positive action. In neither of the above instances can the required policy be achieved by legislation; planning has no control over hours of work, and the dispersal of office accommodation must be on a voluntary basis. The necessary ingredients are enthusiasm backed by an intimate knowledge of the problem, to generate active participation from the public. Perhaps the harnessing of these two forces, neither of which now form part of the official approach to planning, can achieve more for planning in the 1960's than has legislation in the 1950's. Certainly planning resulting from and supported by the strong pressure of public opinion will achieve more than the present apathetic attitude to many of our urgent problems of urban and rural land use.

Conclusion

Population surveys for planning range from the study of individual attitudes and preferences through the impact of group dynamics on land-use requirements to the study of population characteristics and trends within a town or a region as a whole. Population may be

182   SURVEYS FOR TOWN AND COUNTRY PLANNING

regarded as a natural resource and, in this respect, it plays a significant part in planning towards the location of industry: 'Two of our
greatest assets as a nation are the capacity for work and the skill of
our workpeople. It is a national necessity that these assets should be
used to the full. The distribution of industry policy is one means to
this end.[13] It exerts a potent influence through the rate of household
formation on the demands for residential land and ancillary
services. The understanding of social needs and aspirations represents an important and early phase of the urban renewal programme, and an appreciation of attitudes and the response to
conditions in new development is necessary to provide knowledge
which should be applied with advantage in later projects. The study
of population as an integral part of the planning survey illustrates
the concept of planning as a continuous process. Knowledge about
population is fundamental to the preparation of the Development
Plan; the success or otherwise of these intentions should then be
measured in terms of individual and group satisfaction as a guide to
the remedial action which may still be required.

1   Ministry of Housing and Local Government, *Population*, Technical
    Memorandum no. 4, 1955, p. 11 (unpublished).

2   See, for example, A. M. Carr-Saunders, D. Caradog Jones and C. A.
    Moser, *Social Conditions in England and Wales*, 1958, for an evalua-
    tion of national conditions.

3   J. B. Cullingworth, 'Household Formation in England and Wales,
    Town Planning Review, vol. XXXI, no. 1, 1960, pp. 5–26; A. G. Powell,
    The Family Unit, Town and Country Planning Summer School, 1959,
    pp. 89–92.

4   P. Ford and C. J. Thomas, *Housing Targets: Third Report of the
    Southampton Survey*, 1953, appendix I.

5   Ibid, p. 25.

6   Ministry of Housing and Local Government, *Moving from the Slums*,
    H.M.S.O., 1956, p. 3.

7   C. Vereker and J. B. Mays, *Urban Redevelopment and Social Change*,
    1961, p. 117.

8   C. Bauer, *Social Questions in Housing and Town Planning*, 1952, pp.
    9–11.

9 C. Woodbury (ed.), *The Future of Cities and Urban Redevelopment*, 1956, p. 291.

10 Ibid., p. 296.

11 *Annual Report 1960–1961 of the Citizens' Council on City Planning*, *Philadelphia*. See A. Levine, 'Citizen Participation', *The Journal of the American Institute of Planners*, vol. XXVI, 1960, pp. 195–200. Recent American discussion of the opportunities provided by Citizen Participation includes Sears, Roebuck and Co. *Citizens in Urban Renewal*; National Federation of Settlements and Neighbourhood Centres, *Dynamics of Citizen Participation*, 1958; W. C. Loring, *Community Organization for Citizen Participation in Urban Renewal*, 1957; American Society of Planning Officials, *Citizens Planning Groups*, 1961; American Council to Improve our Neighbourhoods (Action), *Citizen Organization for Community Improvement* and *Organization of Block Groups for Neighbourhood Improvement*; and publications (miscellaneous) of the Community Planning Association of Canada.

12 Ministry of Transport, *Crush Hour Travel in Central London*, H.M.S.O., 1958

13 Board of Trade, *Distribution of Industry*, Cmd 7540, 1948.

CONCLUSION

THE text has discussed certain methods of approach to planning surveys which are either currently in use or which might be adopted. Many specialized studies such as shopping or recreational needs, the spheres of influence of towns, or the specific problems of tourist centres have received scant or no mention, but sufficient examples have been provided to indicate the application of the scientific method in the elucidation of planning problems. Planning decisions exert substantial consequences on the individual, the community and the nation for decades hence. Such major decisions for the use and development of land by and on behalf of society must be based on the best available assessment of the evidence which can be obtained through a methodical study of the problem in question. The argument is not survey and research for its own sake, but for its contribution to a greater understanding of environment and of man's impact on its form, character and quality.

Dr Lichfield's concept of the Development Balance Sheet provides a valuable means whereby all the survey knowledge about a given situation can be brought together to assist in making the planning decision. 'When a planning authority is weighing up the advantages and disadvantages of incorporating into its plan a particular development programme or proposal, or one in a particular form, or considering a development application, its outlook is not that of the developer. Its horizon of interest is wider and its objectives different. It must hold the balance between all developers; and between them and the local and national interest. In other words, the implications of a particular proposal that weigh with the developer, and which he will list in preparing his development balance sheet, are not necessarily those which will weigh with the planning authority. There is, in other words, what we will call a 'planning balance sheet'.[1]

184

These arguments also apply at the national and the regional levels of comprehension. The Ministry of Transport or the Ministry of Power are developers when undertaking road improvements schemes or determining the route of an overhead cable. The road and the power lines are their major concern. Their attitudes are therefore different from those of the Planning Ministry with responsibility for the impact of these proposals on adjoining and regional land use. In the field of industrial location a snowball series of repercussions extends from the policy decision to develop into the attraction of population to the area and the land-use demands from associated industries, public utilities, transport and highway requirements. Planning, nationally and locally, involves a full appreciation of the proposed development in all its manifold aspects, economic and social, tangible and intangible, on the community concerned.

The concept of a development balance sheet may also be extended by assessing the gains and losses to the community *after* the development has taken place. It should be used to assess the extent to which the land-use pattern has developed as anticipated. Planning will never be an exact science and precise forecasts of future possibilities are not attainable, but the gap between guesswork and prediction needs to be reduced through a continuous series of studies to promote a greater understanding of the issues involved. This approach is applicable when departments either of national or of local government are involved in the decision to use or to develop land. The total impact of a new motorway, an industrial project, the electrification of a suburban railway line, the siting of a power station, a housing project or the location of a car park are amenable to the same form of consistent analysis. The greater community implications of all developments require to be appreciated if consistency and co-ordination in the use and development of land are to be achieved.

It is the range and complexity of our national problems of land use, so manifest in the quality and condition of our towns, which has ushered in the need for planning. Any form of comprehensive approach towards moulding this environment in some preconceived manner must be based on an understanding of the problems to be solved and the objectives of action. This is the essential contribution of surveys within the greater planning process.

The final word must be that reading can only guide and assist. Problems must be studied in their reality, and no amount of writing about the method of approach to surveys will resolve the deficiencies in knowledge which exist. The reader must pursue his investigations in the field and apply his findings to the solution of real problems. When he has reached the stage of conclusions and recommendations, his greater task still lies ahead. We may remind ourselves that Florence Nightingale wrote in the margin of her reports, 'Reports are not self executive.' The fight for improvement is only in its infancy when the facts are known. Planning requires surveys primarily as a basis for responsible and positive action. 'She wrote the sentence again and again, in a private note, in a letter, on scraps of paper: *Reports are not self executive.*'[2]

1   N. Lichfield, *Economics of Planned Development*, Estates Gazette, 1956.
2   Cecil Woodham-Smith, *Florence Nightingale*, 1952, p. 241.

INDEX

1. Subjects

2. References

ABRAMS, C., 28
Air Ministry, 106
Alexandersson, G., 169
Alston, H. F., 149
American Council to Improve Our Neighbourhoods, 183
American Public Health Association, 128
American Society of Planning Officials, 183
Association for Planning and Regional Reconstruction, 107, 149

BAILEY, D., 59
Barlow Commission, 28
Bauer, C., 182
Beecham, A., 170
Bellamy, J., 59
Berry, B. J. L., 60
Best, R. H., 84
Bestor, G. C., 60
Board of Trade, 60, 183
Bow Group, 28
Bowley, M., 59
Buchanan, C. D., 149
Bureau of Public Roads, 60

CARR-SAUNDERS, A. H., 182
Carter, C. F., 59
Cassie, W. F., 149
Central Office of Information, 28
Chandler, T. J., 107
Chapin, F. S., 28

Charlesworth, G., 149
Chisholm, M., 107
Clark, D. A., 60
Coburn, J. M., 149
Coleman, A., 107
Collins, B. J., 28
Collison, R. L., 59
Conzen, M. R. G., 128
Council of Planning Librarians, 60
Cox, P., 59
Cullingworth, J. B., 182

DAVIES, E., 149
Dawson, R. F. F., 149 (2)
Daysh, G. H. J., 128
Detroit Metropolitan Area, 150
Devons, E., 59
Duncan, A. R., 106

EASTWOOD, T., 170
Economist Intelligence Unit, 170
Estall, R. C., 169

FISHER, R. A., 83
Florence, F. S., 60, 170
Ford, P., 182
Forestry Commission, 60
Freeman, T. W., 29

GARNETT, A., 106
Garrison, W. L., 150
Geddes, Sir P., 29

NITED Nations Housing and Town and Country Planning Bulletin, 28
.S. Dept. of Agriculture, 60

EREKER, C., 182

ARD, J. T., 107

ATES, F., 83

IEBICKI, F., 106